LETT IT GO

ATTAINING AWARENESS OUT OF ADVERSITY

Bev Aisbett

HarperCollins*Publishers*

HarperCollins*Publishers*

First published in Australia in 1996
Reprinted in 1998, 1999, 2000, 2001
by HarperCollins*Publishers* Pty Limited
ABN 36 009 913 517
A member of the HarperCollins*Publishers* (Australia) Pty Limited Group
www.harpercollins.com.au

HarperCollinsPublishers
25 Ryde Road, Pymble, Sydney, NSW 2073, Australia
31 View Road, Glenfield, Auckland 10, New Zealand
77-85 Fulham Palace Road, London W6 8JB, United Kingdom
Hazelton Lanes, 55 Avenue Road, Suite 2900, Toronto, Ontario M5R 3L2
and 1995 Markham Road, Scarborough, Ontario M1B 5M8, Canada
10 East 53rd Street, New York NY 10022, USA

National Library of Australia Cataloguing-in-Publication data:

Aisbett, Bev.
 Letting IT Go: attaining awareness out of adversity.
 ISBN 0 7322 5729 8.
 1. Self-perception. 2. Self-esteem. 3. Life skills.
 4. Self-actualization (Psychology). I. Title.
158.1

Cover illustration by Bev Aisbett
Printed and bound in Australia by Griffin Press on 79gsm Bulky Paperback White

10 9 8 7 6 5   01 02 03 04

Dedicated,
with love,
to Buzzy
for being there in the dawn
that made the darkness all
worthwhile
♥

AND
Deepest thanks for love, friendship,
support & gentle guidance, to
Robbi Zeck, David Milligan
and all at IVI

FOREWORD

Writing the `IT Books', as I fondly refer to them, has offered me great rewards:

- firstly, the privilege of seeing my own creativity immortalised;
- secondly, being in a position to offer hope and help to others through passing on all that I have learned – a great reward indeed;
- and thirdly, to see before me the very evidence of my own evolutionary course of discovery that began with survival, moved through understanding and has now embarked onto insight.

None of these gifts would have come my way if I had not had an **IT**, if I had not experienced what I saw at the time as great suffering.

It was through this very suffering that I was forced to face the fears that I could no longer ignore, work at the resistances I held, clear the blocks that stood in my way and heal the wounds that caused me such pain.

And, as a result, a profound change occurred. I became more aware, more conscious, more enlightened than I had ever been before.

In my quest to overcome what seemed to be an enormous obstacle, I was given the opportunity and the motivation to **change** the way I **lived**.

And so, I once again pass on to you all that I have discovered, in the hope that you too, may find your own answers and finally, peacefully, joyfully, let **IT** go.

Bev Aisbett

CONTENTS

A SPECIAL NOTE
FOR READERS
WITHOUT
PANIC PROBLEMS

The fact that you have not suffered severe anxiety, depression or any other major emotional crisis, does not exclude you from benefiting greatly from the information and exercises contained in this and the two previous books.

Few of us go through life without *some* form of **IT**, whether **IT** be addiction, dependence, illness, anger, impatience, intolerance or one of a myriad other problems around self-worth that hold us back from a true expression of self, or a greater freedom to participate fully and joyfully in life.

Someone suffering from extreme anxiety does not necessarily need to change and grow to any greater degree than many others - the need is just more *urgent*.

I invite you to follow the lead of those wonderful panic people who, in courageously facing their fears and blocks, have worked to rebuild their lives, not only to ensure recovery from anxiety, but to become more loving, independent, compassionate and responsible citizens of the world.

Thank you

THE LAST **IT** BITS

Where are you now?

So, **IT**'s still **around**, eh?

But boy, hasn't he changed!

He's gone from *this* ...   to *this* ...

... or even *this*!

IT has evolved from being a major obstacle to become
an occasional **annoyance** or, hopefully, **a tool for growth**!
And it's all through *your* hard work!!

CONGRATULATIONS!

Look how far you've come!

You've gone from
being **overwhelmed**
by **IT** ...

... to living with **IT**!

In order to achieve this,
you took back control by ...

- accepting ownership
  of your **IT**

- recognising self-defeating
  patterns in your thinking

- monitoring and halting
  negative self-talk

- realising that fear
  did not stop you
  from functioning.

And, having completed your work in these areas, you
moved on to ...

... living **IT** up!

This meant ...

- recognising **IT** in all of **IT's** forms - anger, guilt, self pity - anything that stood in the way of your enjoyment of life

- seeing **IT** as a barometer for the blocks that need work

- not resisting **IT** but working *with* **IT** to instigate positive changes.

And, if you *have* done your homework, by now you probably will have developed ...

- greater self-worth
- a more flexible attitude to life's changes

- more positive self-supporting life choices
- a greater acceptance of others and self
- an increased ability to live in the present.

If not ... sorry, roll up those sleeves and keep working at it!

(I *never* said it was **easy**!!)

Here's a **before** and **after** comparison. These are the changes you might have made to your thinking by now. How do you rate?

BEFORE IT

AFTER IT

I should have done better!
I musn't be late!
I can't do that!

I gave it my best shot!
I'll get there when I can!
I could try and see!

NOW! Rigid, limiting words seldom (if ever!) appear in your vocabulary. You are conscious of the words you choose.

You're wrong!

Well, I see it differently!

NOW! In a conflict situation, you take responsibility for **your** position only and choose `I' statements instead of levelling blame and criticism at others.

Oh no! Another disaster! This is too much! I can't cope!

Hmm... how can I fix this? Where am I stuck?

NOW! You've stopped fretting, complaining and dramatising about your problems. When you encounter a problem, you get on with seeking a solution.

BEFORE IT AFTER IT

NOW! You've stopped negating, apologising for, **comparing** and **putting down** yourself (and others).

NOW! You've stopped blaming luck, God, fate or others for your problems. You take **active steps** to improve your situation instead of wishing problems would magically disappear by themselves.

By **NOW!** quite simply, you feel **better!**

13

If even **half** of these improvements are in place, then surely **IT** has served a **positive** function!

IT has given you the **incentive** to make the changes necessary to give you a **better outlook on life**!

Think back. Remember how **NEGATIVE** you were? How weighed down by pain, worry, fear, anger and trouble?

Can you honestly say that, without **IT**, you would have put in the **effort** required to turn all that around?

But **IT**s work is now over. It's time for ...

LETTING IT GO!

Thanks for the lesson! BYEEE!

Hurrumph!. I know when I'm not wanted!

And this involves ...

- understanding where **IT** began
- seeing the **BIG PICTURE** of your struggle
- making peace with the past
- developing a loving attitude
- releasing fear, anger and negativity
- becoming more focused and conscious
- trusting your own wisdom
- living in the present.

In order to do this, you will need to **really work** at the following:

1 HONESTY

Hmm... am I playing control games here?

The first key to freedom is in being **honest** with yourself. **Really honest.** To effectively remove the cheap drama from your life, you will need to identify when **you** are playing a part in it and face that.

To have **trust** in yourself, you will need to know that you do not rely on **tricks** to get by. This requires courage.

2 IDENTIFYING YOUR BLOCKS

Another headache! I get one every time I visit Mother! Why?

You are a whole human being. Your responses, reactions and resistances have an impact on **all** areas of your life, including your health and your circumstances. Identifying and taking responsibility for your blocks will give you valuable insights for growth.

3 GETTING OUT OF YOUR COMFORT ZONES

Yeow! That hit the spot!!

To fully free yourself, you will need to be prepared to address your fears, anger, blocks and resistances. This can be painful, especially as they become more obvious the more you work at clearing them. But the pay-off is worth it. No pain - no gain! How **much** are you prepared to do to feel better?

4 PATIENCE AND PERSEVERANCE

Boy, it's hard to keep going!

And all of this will require that you hang in there! **Half** a commitment to success will only give you half-baked results! Many people stop short just when they are on the verge of **BREAKING THROUGH**! Stay with it!

So, let's begin with honesty, and take a look at where you are now.

Complete this questionnaire by filling in the percentage.

		% YES	% NO
I AM WHERE I WANT TO BE IN:	My work	50	50
	My homelife	66	33
	Relationships	40	60
I FEEL NURTURED AND SUPPORTED BY:	My friends	75	25
	My family	80	20
	My partner	–	–
	My workmates	50	50
WHEN DEALING WITH OTHERS, I FEEL MOSTLY:	Intimidated	25	25
	Defensive	60	40
	Judgemental		60
	Equal	50	50
	Superior	60	40
	Inferior	50	50
I HAVE IDENTIFIED MY LIFE'S PURPOSE		60	
I ASK FOR WHAT I WANT WITHOUT USING :	Charm	10	
	Ultimatum	25	
	Helplessness	90	
	Hints	75	
	Threats	95	
	Put-downs	90	
IF SOMEONE HAS SUCCESS, I FEEL:	Happy	90	26
	Envious	40	
	Competitive	40	
	Resentful	10	
	Sorry for self	0	
IF SOMEONE NEEDS HELP, I AM LIKELY TO:	Educate them	50	
	Rescue them	75	
	Give advice	50	
	Ask what they need	60	
	Retreat	20	

I TRY TO CHANGE OTHERS	30
I LIVE IN THE PAST	10

I SEE PROBLEMS AS:

■ *Challenges needing solutions*	80	
■ *Punishments*	10	
■ *My bad luck*	30	
■ *Opportunities*	80	

I AM EASILY ABLE TO FORGIVE PERCEIVED SLIGHTS	50
I FEEL HARD DONE BY	10
PEOPLE UNDERSTAND ME	40 ✗
I RELY ON OTHERS' OPINION OF ME TO FORMULATE MY OWN OPINION OF SELF	70

I OFTEN CRITICISE:

■ *Others*	40	
■ *Authorities*	80	
■ *Myself*	60	

I GIVE MORE THAN I GET BACK	50
MY OWN JUDGEMENT IS TRUSTWORTHY	80
I WOULD RATHER BE ALONE THAN IN A RELATIONSHIP THAT IS NOT ABSOLUTELY 50/50	20

I CAN GET ALL THE SUPPORT, NURTURING, ATTENTION AND LOVE I NEED WITHOUT

■ *Struggle*	30	
■ *IT*	90	
■ *Ill health*	60	
■ *Addiction*	30	
■ *Being perfect*	90	
■ *Being indispensible*	90	
■ *Being dependent*	60	
■ *Being special*	20	✗

I LIKE WHO I AM AND WOULD NOT WANT TO BE ANYONE ELSE	75 ✗

Thank you. Your answers will reveal the areas you need to work on.

OK, on the following pages we will begin working towards letting **IT** go.

> In order to proceed, I would now like to introduce you to some exciting **POSSIBILITIES!**

> This will require you to open up to some **NEW THINKING**, but, hey, you've already done a lot of that by now, haven't you?

> No matter how unfamiliar this may seem, I can **GUARANTEE** you this... that if you begin to live out these possibilities, you **WILL** feel better! Worth a try, eh?

Here they are ...

- The purpose of this physical experience – life – is to **learn**. It's *supposed* to be challenging!
- All events have a purpose. Everything has a reason.
- All the wisdom, peace, strength and love you need is already inside you.
- You are not given more than you can handle(!).
- A painful situation or pattern will repeat until it is resolved and cleared.
- Each of us is working from a different script, but working towards the same goal.
- All suffering arises from our own attitude to suffering.
- Wisdom cannot be achieved by an intellectual exercise alone. It can only come from **experience**.
- Your body is no more than a vehicle for **YOU**.
- Everything is connected. Anything is possible.
- What you **believe** will happen, probably will.
- Love is an antidote to all suffering.

BELIEVE IT OR NOT?

The role of a belief system in recovery

The pioneer of psychology, Carl Jung, made an interesting observation. People under his care who had a **spiritual context** to their lives were more likely to experience recovery from emotional breakdown than those who didn't. Why would this be so?

The dictionary defines `spirit' as `the force or principle of life that animates the body of living things'.

So, one might surmise that to have a `spiritual context' in one's life would be to have a meaning for life based on the existence of this greater force.

How might this be helpful to someone suffering from, say, anxiety or depression?

In times of distress particularly, we search for a meaning for our suffering.

We look for a source of help in dealing with our problems. We reach out for comfort and understanding.

Without a reason for our distress, we feel stuck, lost, powerless and unable to move on.

There seems to be no pattern or logic to the events in our lives. We stumble along, hoping for the best, but fearing the worst.

When `bad' things happen to us, we tend to allocate responsibility for our hardship in one of the following ways ...

1 OURSELVES
We either take responsibility or bear the burden of blame.

2 OTHERS
We allocate blame outside ourselves, because we don't have to face or solve a problem we don't *own*.

3 DIVINE JUDGEMENT
We perceive we are being rewarded or punished for our virtues or sins accordingly.

4 LUCK
We attribute events and circumstances to chance - no one's responsibility and no control, either.

And, whether you feel safe or vulnerable, judged or accepted, and whether the Universe is a friendly or hostile place for you, will be governed by your **spiritual view**, and this, in turn, will have been highly influenced by your conditioning and upbringing. Let's take the idea of God, for instance.

For you, God may be ...

A PARENT   As a **parent**, God may be loving or punishing, reflecting your own parents' behaviour towards you when you were growing up.

AN AUTHORITY FIGURE

Vengeful or rewarding, capricious or supportive, depending on your experience of higher authorities, this idea of God will set the rules and operate as a governing force to be feared and revered.

This idea of God will again reflect how much nurture and support you received. This God may not be there for you when you need Him, or may not exist at all for you.

ABSENT

Or, God may be more abstract for you ...
- a Divine Energy
- a Transcendental Force
- a Natural Order.

All of this will affect your world view and your sense of worth and safety.

BASICALLY-

If you have high self-esteem you are more likely to perceive a safe Universe governed by a loving force.

If your self-esteem is low the Universe will feel threatening and you will anticipate punishment for mistakes.

So, we can see from this that an individual's spirituality and psychology are so closely linked as to be two sides of the same coin.

And, given this, your idea of **spirituality** will also be highly coloured by your **experience** of **religion** in your upbringing.

But aren't RELIGION and SPIRITUALITY one and the same?

Not really. Let's turn to the dictionary again for a definition of `religion'.

RELIGION: `A formal or institutionalised expression of belief in divine powers.'

Religion involves a set of **rituals** and **practices** that **connect** us to the **spiritual.**

OMM...

So, it could be argued that **spirit,** this `force', exists, whether we practice **religion** (i.e. connect with it) or not!

In fact, many people have become disillusioned by the conventional Church. Here are some of their views:

I always leave church feeling guilty - like I'm a sinner. I don't feel good about myself!

I can't figure out how we can kill others in the name of God! It's hypocritical!

The idea of a loving God doling out eternal punishment doesn't make sense!

People in my religion seem to feel theirs is the only way and that others are wrong. Isn't that judgmental?

If I'm such a **hopeless sinner,** I'll probably end up **damned.** If so, how can I feel **good** about life?

My mother used to say 'God will get you for this!' Religion meant fear and guilt for me!

We turn to religion, or a belief system, to find a purpose for our lives, a reason for our suffering, as well as a hope for the future.

If the belief system you have adopted does not satisfy these criteria, does not leave you feeling supported and nurtured, then perhaps your *beliefs* need to be re-examined.

ABOUT BELIEFS

Back to the dictionary again.
To `believe' is `to accept as true ... to think, assume, suppose.'

Our *beliefs* can be erroneous.

You're a DUD! You're STUPID! You'll never get rid of me!

You believed all the stuff **IT** told you didn't you?

We all **BELIEVED** the Earth was **FLAT**, didn't we?

So, how were these **beliefs** changed?

WE EXPERIENCED OTHERWISE!

Here's Fred — Women are inferior to men!

and here's Harry. — Women are our equals!

Both these men have **beliefs**. They arrived at their vastly different beliefs through different experiences and perceptions. For both Fred and Harry, this is the *truth*. For either to change their beliefs, they will need to experience otherwise, and in order to change, they will have to become dissatisfied with their current experience or transformed by a new experience.

Many people, having experienced a lack of fulfilment through the beliefs espoused by one religion, tend to turn their backs completely on the pursuit of *any* spiritual life.

What may need to be questioned, however, is not spirituality, per se, but rather, this one particular approach to it.

Cultures throughout the world adopt widely varying means to exploring and accessing a spiritual path, and the system you were brought up with is only *one* of them. The goal, however, remains the same - union with a Divine force, and as such, a return to our original perfection.

But whatever path you choose, your physical, mental and emotional life will be greatly enhanced by developing a spiritual outlook.

HOW? Well, let's look at what having a spiritual outlook might mean.

☆ We accept that the force that manages to keep a whole Universe in balance might just be better at running things than we are!

When I try to control everything, everything goes out of control!

☆ We accept change, rather than permanence, as the natural way.

I'll just see what happens next!

☆ We begin to move *with* change rather than insisting on our own desired outcomes.

☆ We stop labelling experiences as `good' or `bad', instead seeing each situation as part of the full experience of life.

Nope, I ain't bending!

☆ We recognise that the same energy that constitutes all of life, is not **outside** us, but is housed **within** us, connecting us to each other, and all living things.

Most major cultures employ metaphors, fables and myths to explain the workings of things and to simplify concepts. Here is a new one to help explain the above points and how you fit in ...

25

The Journey

There was (and still is) a vast, knowing, utterly balanced, perfect energy called **THE SOURCE**.

THE SOURCE contained all of the ingredients that were to become you and me, trees, cars, even nuclear bombs ... **everything**, but at this stage these things were just **possibilities**, for then **THE SOURCE** had no form. It was just pure energy, playing through space, and we were part of it.

And, because everything connected to **THE SOURCE** was in perfect balance, there was complete knowing and harmony ...

Then, one day the energy that was to

YAHOO!

become you and me, spotted something called the **physical plane**!

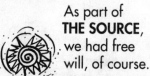

As part of **THE SOURCE**, we had free will, of course.

This is cool! —Yeah!

... But the only way to stay on the **physical plane** was to take to a **physical form** ...

Hey, great outfit!

Thanks! Yours too!

So we decided to explore this **physical plane**.
   ... Thereby removing ourselves from **THE SOURCE**!

And, of course, what we had chosen was **LIFE**, and *all* of its experiences ...

OW! This hurts!

But by now, we had completely forgotten our **SOURCE**. We totally believed that we could control everything, and think and fight and invent our way out of this mess.

What was that?

And so we trudged on, lifetime after lifetime, repeating the same mistakes, until, finally, we caught a glimpse of what we'd had all along ...

All we had to do to reconnect with **THE SOURCE** was to **remember** its energy was within us, but we soon forgot. We decided we knew better. After all, we had **free will**, and this was our choice.

JOY   SORROW   PAIN   SEX

FEAR   HATRED   LOVE   AND DEATH

Soon, we discovered that, though the good bits of life were great, the bad bits could hurt us badly. We had trouble handling life.

I know! I'll make a new form of power!

Whoops!

We had forgotten how to connect with all the peace, balance, wisdom, strength and power we began with.

... and by clearing away all the negativity and illusion, we revealed a treasure that lay within us - **THE SOURCE** - our own true selves.

What could this mean to you?

Perhaps this is just a story. Or perhaps it's not!
Let's review some of the possibilities that appear on page 18.

• LIFE IS EDUCATION.
LIFE IS CHALLENGING.

If we have lost sight of our original perfection, then we have to address our blocks to this perfection. This means pain whenever we hit those blocks. We will do this many times before learning to clear them. We're slow learners.

• ALL YOU NEED IS INSIDE YOU.

May **THE SOURCE** be with you!
The same energy that makes the grass grow, the wind blow and the sun shine, makes you tick as well! You just need to learn how to *access* it! And, for every handicap you have, you possess a compensatory strength. Are you using it?

• ALL EVENTS HAVE A PURPOSE.

I need to learn patience!

Where you are at is exactly where you need to be to learn whatever you need to learn. Pain is a great motivator. Look back over your life. When did you learn the most? When you were happy or when you were challenged?

• YOU ARE NOT GIVEN MORE THAN
YOU CAN HANDLE.

Feels that way! But the minute you *choose* to handle something, you do! We have **free will**.
Some people survive hideous circumstances and come out smiling. Some people kill themselves over a broken love affair!
Choice.
You can go with it and grow. Give in and you'll never know.

- **A PAINFUL SITUATION WILL REPEAT TILL CLEARED.**

If you do what you've always done, you'll get what you've always got. Did you `get it' last time or just blunder back in and hope it will turn out better by doing the *same*? You are not being **punished**. You are being **educated**. Clear the block and move on.

- **SUFFERING IS AN ATTITUDE.**

There is no `punishment' or `reward'. `Punishment' arises from our own resistances and holding of pain. The `reward' comes from living *any* experience *well*. Life is not about `good' or `bad' experiences - just **contrasts**. We label experiences good or bad according to our **perception** of them. In fact, there is no prize, no goal to be reached! The journey ends where it began ... with your true self, until now buried under illusions and pain.

- **EACH OF US HAS A DIFFERENT SCRIPT.**

If we consider that we're all on a journey back to our perfection, then some people will be further along with their lessons than others. Don't judge! Someone may be figuring out raw physical strength, while someone else may be working on material or mental lessons. Their scripts are just *different* from yours, but no less (or more) valid.

- **WISDOM ONLY COMES FROM EXPERIENCE.**

Believing in a spiritual force is not as important as **opening** to it. A purely intellectual approach may give you ideas but only through direct experience will you gain **wisdom**. Listen - your heart's beating. Do you have to **believe** in it for it to do so? That's how it is with a spiritual energy. If you open to it, you'll experience it. And really, does it matter *where* healing comes from?

QUESTIONS

- Did you grow up in a religious environment?
- If you did, was it a spiritually nourishing environment?
- If you could picture a god, what would he/she/it look like?
- Where do you believe this god abides?
- Does giving a spiritual force a persona limit its power for you? Or enhance it?
- Do you believe in divine punishment or reward? Why?

EXERCISE

Close your eyes and try to picture yourself as pure energy, and your body as just the shell that contains it.

See yourself as an energy that is perfect – balanced, loving, peaceful, timeless, accepting, wise and calm.

Now picture yourself moving through life from this new viewpoint.

How differently would you feel, think or behave?

What would be your attitude towards your body in this context?

MY STORY

One day, during a particularly rough patch, when I was feeling pretty sorry for myself, I got thinking about the above idea. What if I was a spiritual being? How would I behave?

With this in mind, I went to the beach, and decided to try to operate from that level. I became very calm, a little aloof, very wise and dignified.

And suddenly, I also found I had a new appreciation of the water, the rocks, the sun and the air as being forms of energy that fed my own. I no longer felt so alone and powerless. I was part of it all, and everything was exactly as it needed to be.

THIS IS YOUR LIFE

The origins of low self-esteem

So, this is the script you've been given for your journey.

It determines your character - your race, gender, personality, physical and mental qualities and all the challenges that go with these.

It contains many entrances and exits, cues and upstagings. You only receive one page at a time.

How well you perform this page will influence what follows.

And, for this particular drama, **IT** has been written into the script ...

For most of us, he starts out playing the

VILLAIN...

... but he has every chance of becoming the **HERO!**

Meanwhile, however, **IT's** part in the play brings you a challenging role, filled with ALL of life's great dramas ...

FEAR

ANGER

GUILT

ILL HEALTH

... to name but a few!

And at the bottom of these is one common thread ...

LOW SELF-ESTEEM!

Given that this play is all about working through your biggest lessons, we need to go back and find out where this low self-esteem came from and how it figures in the scheme of things.

In order to do this, let's meet the cast ...

THE EXTRAS ...	... THE CAMEO ROLES	THE KEY PLAYERS

These are the 1000s of nameless faces you encounter each day ...	... some of whom will move in and out of your life at a particular time and for a particular reason.	These include family, friends, partners, colleagues and authority figures.

All have a key role and all have been perfectly cast for this drama. Everyone's timing is impeccable, everyone says the right lines on cue, and everyone enters and exits exactly when they should.

And, of course, the **STAR** is...

YOU!

- How will you go?
- Will you fulfil your role?
- Will you figure out the plot?

Let's see ...

CURTAIN UP!
APPLAUSE!
Let's begin!

SCENE 1 – YOUR ARRIVAL

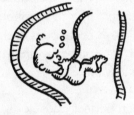

Here you are, snuggly, floating in your mother's belly. You're perfect!!

Then, suddenly, you are catapulted out into the harsh glare of reality ...

... to meet your first key players (and role models) – your parents*.

(*or significant others – elders, authority figures, etc.)

Already, according to *your* script,
there may be snags ...

Your parents might be like this ...   ... or they might be like this!

The influence of your parents and other elders runs very deep. What you learn from them in your developmental years helps to form the patterns and responses of a lifetime.

They are your **role models.**

They give you your view of the world.

That the world is
wonderful and safe...

...or that the world is
corrupt ,evil and dangerous.

They show you what you
might expect from others ...

... and how to behave
towards them.

Support ... or betrayal   with cooperation ... or contempt.

They give you examples of how **love** operates ...

*In other words...
they teach you how
to
"DO" LIFE !*

that love
heals..

or love
hurts.

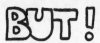 **BUT !** Before we get into **blaming** Mum and Dad ...

I did the best I could with what I had!

Remember that Mum and Dad had *their* scripts to work through too, which dictated *their* particular values and behaviour!

And so did I!

Be generous. What they began with may have been very limited indeed!

But whatever they were like, they were perfectly cast for you to learn what you most need to (as you will see)!

So according to everyone's **key players** and **role models**, things proceed to plan.

For a while, at least, everything may look rosy ...

You are the
CENTRE
of the
UNIVERSE!

All of your needs are met
and all you have to do
to get attention
is *scream*!!
(Sound familiar?)

There is no question about your worth or lovability. You are perfect simply because you exist. You don't have to **please.** You are fully self-absorbed.

Then, as time goes by, you begin to become aware of the outside world and your unique place in it.

You start to become an **individual.**

This can be a rough transition.

For a start, you feel like **exploring** ...

... and for the first time you encounter the idea of being **wrong**.

The messages begin to become more and more mixed. You are compelled to explore this new world and your territory ... but this can bring trouble.

You begin to wonder if you can be yourself, be independent, be an individual ...

... and still be **loved**!

Just how tricky this transition is will depend on a lot of factors involving your parents.

• THEIR OWN SCRIPTS

Your parents inherited issues from *their* parents. Perhaps they had worked through these issues, perhaps not. Quite possibly, they had never even thought of having 'issues', and so, in ignorance, the legacy goes on.

• HOW LOVING THEY WERE

Your parents may not have shown physical affection and you felt un-nurtured. They may have been violent and you felt unloved. Or they may have been so over-protective that you felt smothered.

• THEIR ATTITUDE TO DISCIPLINE

Again, this will have been greatly influenced, not only by how heavily disciplined they themselves were when growing up, but also by the popular thinking of the time.

In essence, the ease with which you evolved into your own person will have been affected by how many **rules** you had to live by in order to be accepted.

Scene 2 - Society

 But you may have been fortunate. Your script may have allowed for your earliest days to be filled with unconditional love and acceptance ...

... and full of confidence, you began to move out into the world ...

... only to discover that fitting into society added a whole new set of demands and restraints.

Aspects of your behaviour, once praised as lovable, suddenly became unacceptable ...

DON'T RUN! STOP THAT! SPEAK UP! DON'T DAWDLE! BE QUIET!

You were suddenly confronted with a confusing and conflicting set of messages that told you how to be, how to act and what to think.

See? They're pink!

... like showing your knickers ...

Mummy, that lady's FAT!

... or being too `honest'

In order to be **accepted** you learned to **conform** ...

... and, in **conforming** you began to lose your spontaneity.

To fit in, you had to squash down what was once your natural expression of self. (And, to a child, even small things are significant.)

The message, loud and clear was ...

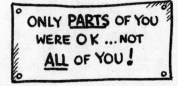

ONLY **PARTS** OF YOU WERE O K ... NOT **ALL** OF YOU !

By now, you will have had to do a lot of **improvising** to navigate this obstacle course into self-worth and self-reliance.

Other factors in your script will have also affected your degree of success in this. Some of these are:

• YOUR PERSONALITY

You may have an easy-going temperament and laugh off problems, or you may be very practical and able to reason your way through.

You may be sensitive and easily hurt. You may be led by your emotions.

• YOUR PHYSICAL APPEARANCE

Like it or not, our society worships physical beauty and bodily perfection. If you were at all `different' growing up, life would have been more challenging for you.

• YOUR ENVIRONMENT

Children should be seen and not heard!

Perhaps you came from a strict upbringing ...

Where are the kids?

Dunno... doin their own thing, I guess!

... or a somewhat *laissez faire* environment.

There may have been cultural restrictions ...

Of course you can't! You're a girl!

Or generational differences ...

No, you can't listen to that! Modern music is rubbish!

... or religious/political beliefs.

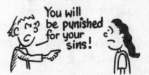

You will be punished for your sins!

There may have been financial constraints ...

... or too much emphasis on power or material gain.

• FAMILY HIERARCHY

Depending on where you appeared in the pecking order, you may have encountered problems in your developmental years as a result.

As a first-born, you may have become a junior parent, with responsibilities to your younger siblings.

A middle child may find him/herself vying for attention between the eldest and youngest and feel left out.

The only child, growing up with adults, may miss out on developing self-reliance and independence, or become spoiled and self-indulgent.

The `baby' may remain that – gaining extra attention and expecting this outside the family.

All of these factors make growing into a healthy, balanced totally **OK** adult, at the very least, difficult, if not virtually impossible! No wonder we have **IT**s!

Scene 3 – Enter the villain!

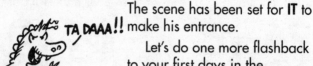

TA DAAA!!

The scene has been set for **IT** to make his entrance.

Let's do one more flashback to your first days in the world.

You were complete. You responded naturally and instinctively. You experienced **wholeness**.

Then, as we saw, any love or acceptance that you received, started to have **conditions** on it.

I'll love you if you're good, don't cry, don't embarass me and behave by my rules!

In order to be **OK**, i.e. **acceptable**, certain natural behaviours and responses had to be **suppressed**.

For example:

Playing with yourself was no longer allowed – your natural sexuality was denied

Having a tantrum was not acceptable – your expression of anger was denied.

So, if you encountered a lot of rules in your formative years about what was acceptable and if your feelings were not acknowledged or allowed expression, more and more parts of you would have had to be disowned, in order for you to fit in. The things that you could no longer own became

The Buried Self

The **BURIED SELF** is like a cupboard into which we place certain thoughts, feelings and behaviours that are not approved of or encouraged.

Into this cupboard go natural behaviours we have to suppress, and with this goes our natural expression of self.

We also store away aptitudes that we have had to deny, and so we grow up believing that we can't achieve in certain areas - can't be strong, for instance, or are not good at sports, as another example, or can't draw, etc., because abilities were suppressed in these areas.

So, how does **IT** fit in here?

 Well, inevitably, there will be times when you forget and do the very thing that is not allowed ...

 When suddenly, you are aware of the voice of authority in your head, telling you this is **bad**!

 And with that comes a jolt of anxiety - enter **IT** stage left.

 Too many of these and you begin to become anxious about doing *anything*.

You become afraid to **be yourself**. Being yourself **hurts**. You present a cardboard cut-out of yourself to the world – a false presentation of yourself that is acceptable to others.

This compensatory mask can have its own drawbacks. For instance:

 If your childhood lacked affection ...

... you may cut yourself off from the longing for affection by completely *rejecting* it ...

... and, as a result, you are perceived as someone who is cold, hard or aloof ...

 ... which can bring you even more hurt!

More and more goes into the cupboard as we struggle to fit in.

More and more we lose touch with our original wholeness.

It becomes harder and harder to contain these stored emotions and frustrations. It becomes harder and harder to maintain the false image that we have erected. Little bits begin to pop out, in tears, anger, resentment, and anxiety.

Eventually ... we feel **bad** enough to face the issue.

And it is at this point, that the true **HEALING** can begin.

QUESTIONS

- What do you think is the greatest lesson you need to learn from your life?
- What does your parents' example tell you about the way you live your life?
- If your parents are perfectly scripted to bring about necessary change in you, how so?
- Listen to your parent's voice in your head. What does it say?
- Do you have a dream? Are you working to fulfil it?

EXERCISE

Compile a list of your parents' better qualities and their shortcomings.

Now compile a list of your own.

In what ways do they match?

In what ways do they differ?

MY STORY

My parents had lost a daughter before I was born, and my mother was very ill when she was carrying me, to the degree that abortion was considered.

With only one sibling twelve years older than me, I grew up virtually as an only child surrounded by adults.

My struggle as an adult was to overcome dependency, not to fear solitude and to trust my own judgement.

I learned to hide these `shortcomings' by *appearing* to be strong-willed, direct and fiercely independent.

STUMBLING BLOCKS

Recognising blocks to recovery

So– To begin **HEALING**, we must first begin to recognise the **blocks** that stand in the way of this healing.

Doing this is similar to peeling away the layers of an onion, and can produce just as many tears in the process.

But what you are about to peel away, in this and the next few chapters, are all the layers of defence; the barricades that have kept you locked up in anxiety and frustration. The energy that it has taken to hold the **BURIED SELF** at bay has been enormous. Now you are ready to take the next step: the return to your true, whole self.

DON'T BE AFRAID TO FEEL

Keeping a lid on your emotions may have made you socially acceptable, but in so doing, you have created a pressure cooker inside. These feelings then tend to pop out in other ways - in grouchiness, tearfulness, resentment, and, of course, panic attacks!

The interesting thing is, these little outbursts alienate you even more!

So, our first efforts must be to identify these blocks and set about clearing them to allow true healing to occur.

It is time to tell the truth to yourself.

For years you have bought an image of yourself that has been distorted, as you will have seen by listening in to **IT**.

As a result, many of us are unfamiliar with who we really are, and by choosing to live with integrity, we must be prepared to shed light on the `difficult' parts of ourselves.

Jung calls this part of ourselves that holds our fears and pain, **`THE SHADOW'**.

Walking *towards* the Shadow can lead to a difficult period, but great freedom lies beyond.

In your preparedness to live truthfully, it becomes harder to support the lies and deceptions of your old thinking, and as a result, a heightened awareness of these blocks throws them into stark relief.

This can sometimes be a humbling and somewhat painful experience.

Yikes! I was being manipulative!

But you are aiming to become more **ENLIGHTENED** and enlightenment means casting a **light on**, clearing out the dark spots within. Turn a light on and darkness disappears!

Enlightenment can also mean becoming **lighter**: less burdened and free of the baggage that has weighed you down for a lifetime, so that you can finally get on with **real** living!

Clearing out your blocks means being prepared to step out of your comfort zone in order to grow.

It means discovering ways of having *your* needs met, of nurturing *yourself*, of looking after *yourself*, by *yourself*. It means recognising that no one else can (or should) do this as well as *you* can!

So, let us begin, but first:

REMEMBER

This is not about YOU being unacceptable!
It is about the things that are STUCK being unacceptable.

Introducing~

The Catalogue
of
COMMON BLOCKS

PROJECTION

Whatever we can't tolerate inside, we tend to see outside. Projection such as this involves disowning our own feelings and placing them onto another. We do this not only with individuals, but with organisations, authority figures and objects: it's the car's fault, the boss's fault, the government's fault. This places the responsibility elsewhere and absolves us from our responsibility to own our anger, impatience, failings, etc.

HELPLESSNESS

Are you playing the child?

In being helpless, inadequate or ineffectual, we give away our power. By getting someone else to take over, we don't even have to try!

It is up to **you** to instigate your own growth and healing. Part of this *may* involve recruiting the help of others – to help you to **help yourself**.

ORGANISING

Followed by ...

Many of us have a tendency to take over, then resent the extra burden of responsibility! Correcting this involves recognising that others are entitled to live their lives their own way, no matter how this clashes with *your* ideals! If you're into organising or `rescuing', recognise that you are removing another person's right and responsibility to sort out their own lives and make their own mistakes. How does it serve *you* to take over? Does it make you feel needed? Why do you only feel important doing it *this* way?

INVISIBILITY

If you are not being heard or your message is often misunderstood, what does that say about your communication?

- Do you **value** your opinions?
- Do you state your needs clearly or **hope** that people will `just know' what you want?
- Do you **speak up** if something bothers you?
- Do you **expect** to be heard?

DENIAL

It's not my fault! She let me down!

This requires full ownership of *your* stuff.

You will need to recognise your own role in your present circumstances: your own reactions, blocks and limitations.

If you feel let down, put upon, ripped off etc., what part of you **allowed** this to happen?

MISERLINESS

Boy! She gets all the breaks! Why not me?

You think you've got it bad! Well, wait till you hear what happened to me!

How **excited** can you be for another person?

How much joy can you share without getting into *your own* stuff?

Similarly, how much can you give of yourself to another in their suffering without going 'one better' with *your* sad story? Learn to be generous with:

- your time
- your feelings
- your attention
- your deeds

You'll feel better!

MIND-READING

I know what you're thinking!

Actually, you **don't** know what another is thinking.

Ask, don't **assume**.

GIVING

I give and I give... what about me?!

Do you give till it hurts? Why? What if you stopped?

Giving is fine, if the motive is pure. Giving however, can be a device to receive attention, admiration, appreciation or affection in return, and this always backfires.

No one wants a gift with the price tag attached!

EXPECTATIONS

How **crowded** is your life with rules?

The only person you can make rules for is *you*. Having rigid rules for other people's behaviour will leave you constantly frustrated, because people will always deviate from them!

Allow things to unfold - let yourself be surprised by a different outcome to the one you were fixed on.

COERCION

Surrendering this means being clear and direct in asking for what you want without resorting to charm, nagging, blaming, whingeing and sulking, etc. to receive it. **Ask for what** you need and **risk being refused.**

GUILT

Using guilt is another way of **blackmailing** to get what you want. You don't have to play that game! As above, be **direct** in your requests. Don't buy into other people's guilt either. Remind them of what they're doing, and refuse to be part of it.

REGRET

I wish I'd been more patient!

There's only one way to stop regretting, and that's to **stop doing the things that you'll regret**! What's done is done! Recognise the problem and **fix** it.
Don't **agree** to something if you would rather **refuse** it!

PHYSICAL BLOCKS

Often our biggest blocks are apparent in the way that we present ourselves to the world. This is what others see and this affects how people respond to us.

Getting to know yourself better means shedding light on what messages you are giving out about yourself.

1 YOUR VOICE

Listen in to the way that you communicate to others. This can give you valuable clues about your own self-image. What does your voice say about you? Is it clear, strong, calm, centred? What words do you choose? Do you communicate differently with different people? Why?

BABY TALK
Do you sometimes adopt childhood speech or expressions? When do you do this?

DITHERY
Is your speech scattered, hesitant, apologetic, unclear? What is making you unfocused? When do you do this?

BOSSY
Is your speech barking, brash, loud, overbearing? Why do you feel you are not being heard?

WHINING
Is your voice flat, defeated, filled with woes? How do others respond to you? Do you **expect** to be disappointed?

TEARFUL
Is there a quaver, a catch in your throat? What is making you sad?

ANGRY
Are there telltale signs of bitterness or resentment in your voice? What do you need to clear?

MUFFLED

Do you mumble or speak so softly that people ask you to repeat what you have just said? How much value do you place on what you have to say?

SPEEDY

Is your speech in short, sharp, clipped–off statements? Or do you rush on breathlessly? What would happen if you slowed down?

INTERRUPTING

Do you interrupt others often, or finish their sentences for them? Could you benefit from learning more patience? What are you missing?

2 BODY LANGUAGE

STOOPED POSTURE

Often, people with self esteem problems will be hunched over as if they literally carry the weight of the world on their shoulders.?
What happens if you straighten up? What do you feel?

CLOSED SHOP

A closed posture says `keep out' to others. Ask yourself, what is `dangerous' about opening up to life and others.

FIDGETING

How do you feel?
• Impatient?
• Anxious?
• Bored?
Have you found out how to just `BE'?

3 FACE FACTS

What message does your facial expression convey? Is it open, calm, friendly? Is it closed down around pain, hurt, anger? How will your face become `set' when you're older? What would happen to your face if you felt better? What if you smiled more?

4 ACHES AND PAINS

New research in the area of health is recognising what early cultures have understood for centuries - that the body/mind connection is very powerful indeed.

When we look at the possibility of illnesses having an emotional basis, or, at least, a physical vulnerability being aggravated by emotional stress, this opens up a whole new way of understanding what ails us and what our blocks are, and returns us to the power to initiate our own healing.

Here is an overview of the areas of the body and the emotions that may be linked to them. Use this as `food for thought' about your possible blocks.

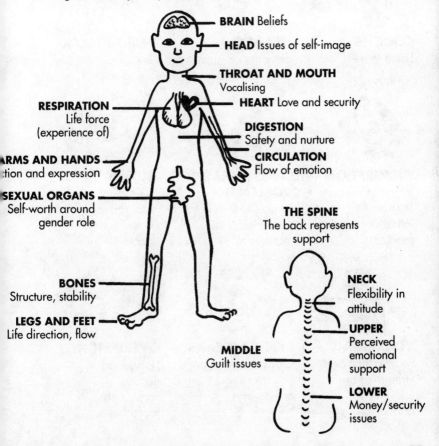

BRAIN Beliefs

HEAD Issues of self-image

THROAT AND MOUTH Vocalising

HEART Love and security

RESPIRATION Life force (experience of)

DIGESTION Safety and nurture

ARMS AND HANDS :tion and expression

CIRCULATION Flow of emotion

SEXUAL ORGANS Self-worth around gender role

THE SPINE The back represents support

BONES Structure, stability

NECK Flexibility in attitude

LEGS AND FEET Life direction, flow

UPPER Perceived emotional support

MIDDLE Guilt issues

LOWER Money/security issues

55

Let's look at some common ailments and see what they tell us.

ANXIETY
Not trusting the flow of life. Resisting change. Accepting powerlessness.

BURNS
Anger. You need to get to the deeper issue.

COLDS, FLU
Overload. Too much going on - a need to shut down.

COUGHS
Listen to me!

HEADACHES
Self-criticism, holding old limitations.

HEART ATTACK
Lack of joy and love. Giving but not receiving.

INDIGESTION
What can't you stomach? What's producing fear?

LUNGS (BREATHING PROBLEMS)
Not able to take in life fully. Holding in, emotionally.

BUMPS
A problem requires your attention. A reminder of blocks.

INSOMNIA
Fear or guilt over unfinished business.

EYES AND EARS
Obvious - what are you avoiding seeing or hearing?

OVERWEIGHT
Using food as nurture. Feeling need for protective padding.

QUESTIONS

- What would you say are your major blocks?
- If a friend were to describe you, what would he/she list as your strengths and weaknesses?
- Where in your body do you hold your fear and pain?
- Which three words would best describe your
  - facial expression
  - physical presentation
  - style of social expression?

EXERCISE

Make a list of the illnesses and ailments you have had. Now study the mannequin on page 55 to assess what areas they relate to emotionally.

Can you see a pattern here?

MY STORY

I was having a bit of a dispute with my partner. We had not resolved it by the time he had to leave for work, and I still felt some anger.

Soon after, I began to do some ironing, when suddenly I burnt my finger, causing a painful blister.

Later in the day, my partner called me. We spoke for some time about the `issue`, until it was finally cleared and peace was restored.

As I hung up, I bumped my finger. Magically, the pain, which had persisted all day, had *gone*!

THE OUCH FACTOR

Using criticism as a tool

CRITICISM

Criticism can leave us feeling exposed and hurt. But criticism, used creatively, can act as an extremely useful device for personal growth and change.
Let's take a look.

Say someone criticises you over something you just *know* you have no problem with ...

... at most, you'll be surprised, because you know you're good at that ...

... but you won't feel hurt. You'll probably shrug it off, thinking your accuser has lost the plot.

Now, let's try a different scenario.

This time, you receive a criticism ...

... and you feel an `ouch'! That **hurt**!

You might react in one of several ways ... angry denial ...

... a return of the same ...

... becoming upset - hoping for a sympathetic retraction ....

... or trying to appear otherwise.

But nonetheless, it hit the spot.

What's the difference between criticism A and criticism B?

Criticism A didn't bother you. You know perfectly well how to cook. It held no meaning for you.

Criticism B, on the other hand, hurt you, because you accepted that it was **true**!!

What was levelled at you hit the spot because it contained a belief you held to be **true** about yourself - otherwise it would have had no effect!

So, what can be done about this?

Well, you need to change your **PERSONAL TRUTH**!
  Let's try that again ...

You could change your idea about what is a 'negative' trait and turn it into a positive one.
  For instance, being 'sensitive' may give you creativity, insight or compassion!

You could work on your 'faults' and find ways to become less 'sensitive'. Perhaps you could think about how you respond to situations and learn not to over-react. Then being 'too sensitive' would no longer apply to you!

CRITICISM can give you vital insights into yourself and others. Remember the **BURIED SELF**?

A fair bit of criticism that is levelled at you may actually have a basis in truth. Try not to react, but take it on board as something to be conscious of, and work at.

Watch for the same criticisms that come up again and again. These may indicate your own unmet childhood needs. In this case, the woman feels overlooked, as she did in childhood.

Criticism that you level at another may actually indicate something you dislike in yourself (that is, something that was disapproved of in childhood). In this case, you may normally be a real fusspot, but very disorganised when it comes to paying bills, paperwork, etc.

This kind of criticism may involve a degree of wish fulfilment. What you criticise most in another may be the very thing you would like to have developed in yourself. In this case, the man may wish he could be more assertive and less compliant.

As we saw in *Living IT up*, however, whatever you criticise most tends to be reinforced in your daily experience.

Suddenly what you dislike ...

... appears to confront you everywhere!

WHY? Because you're **focused** on it!

Now, I'd like to introduce you to an interesting part of your brain.

We'll make this a short introduction, because we get to meet him in depth later.

We'll call him **PRIMAL BRAIN** (or **PB** for short).

Essentially, **PB**'s main concern is survival. He is not terribly sophisticated. His department is the feeling, reacting and responding department. As a result, he's not too fussy about *what* he reacts to - if the impact is great enough, he'll take it on board. He has no sense  of humour, of time, or what is real, fictional or imagined. He just **feels**.

And, so it is with **CRITICISM**.

Feed **PB** criticism, and he'll take it **personally**!

That means *any* criticism ...

of yourself ...

... others ...

... the weather ...

... your car ...

... politicians ...

... **anything**!

Old **PB** takes it on board!

What happens?

You immediately tense up.

Your muscles tighten and *you* begin to feel far worse than whoever (or whatever) you're criticising! Feed yourself enough of this poison (such as the **IT** speak!) and you'll be **guaranteed** of a bad day (and you'll probably complain about that!)

The Antidote?

PRAISE

Remember that **PB**'s not fussy. Whatever has the greatest impact, hits the spot (past or present)! Praise flicks a switch in **PB** and you immediately begin to relax. It doesn't matter *where* the praise is directed – inwardly to yourself or outwardly to others or things or events – it will have a calming effect.

 You don't even have to speak! Just think it. **PB** will hear.

Learn to increase your appreciation of what you like and tolerance of what you don't like.

CRITICISM KILLS
PRAISE HEALS

What if YOU'RE being criticised?

Immediately negate the impact of the criticism by praising yourself. If you don't **fear** criticism it breaks the spell. Make it automatic, like saying 'Bless you' when someone sneezes. **PB** will stay calm and so will you.

'POSITIVE' CRITICISM

Pretty well all criticism levelled at others is self-serving. It deflects attention away from what we cannot tolerate in

 ourselves, or what we do not want revealed to others. To put another down (however 'nicely') gives us a momentary sense of superiority to cover our own inadequacies.

However, if we did not feel threatened, we would not have to win power this way. Sometimes, we genuinely believe our criticism is helpful!

However, there *are* times when we are asked to give an opinion and we'd like to tell the truth. Well, keeping old **PB** and the greatest impact thing in mind, here are some ways to offer feedback.

Usually, as a rule of thumb, **PB** will retain what he's left with *last*.

EXAMPLE 1 THE TURNAROUND
Here is the usual pattern:

PB Just received a wet fish in the face!
Now let's try turning it around.

The advice, given in this way, seems less like criticism. The listener is left with an upper and not a downer.

EXAMPLE 2 THE CUSHION

The effect is softened by surrounding the criticism with praise.

In both cases, the listener is more likely to be open to your view if it is handled with care.

Unfocused Criticism

This type of criticism involves a sweeping statement and an unfocused generality.

Unfortunately, if your self-esteem is low you will tend to assume a guilty position without realising you do not have the full picture of what it is you are feeling guilty about!

Here's an example:

What's your immediate conclusion?

You've jumped straight to the negative assumption!

There are four steps to take in dealing with unfocused criticism:

1 ASK FOR SPECIFICS

What *does* the person **mean**?

The meaning needs to be defined and clarified.

Don't **assume** that you know the meaning. This asks the person making the statement to be clear in their own mind. too.

2 GET OUT OF GUILT

Is this the whole truth or the other person's interpretation?

You have been given a broad statement. Think about it. If you have become more selfish, did you *need* to?

Perhaps *sometimes* you are selfish, but mostly you're a good person. *You* judge (then return to Step 1).

3 OWNERSHIP

Again, this places the onus on the accuser to think about where *they're* coming from. *Whose* problem is it? Ask for clarity.

4 SOLUTION

Invite the person levelling the criticism to come up with a solution. You can **choose** to go along with it or not.

All of this is about being

If you don't know, ask!! Do you have the full picture or just a vague idea? Are you fully **clear** on what is being levelled at you?

And if the answer is still vague, ask again!

BEING CLEAR MEANS
NO GUESSWORK!

Get clear on what is expected. Get answers. **Find out!**

- It is *your* responsibility to get *all* of the information you need.
- It is *your* responsibility to state your limits.
- It is *your* responsibility to make yourself heard and understood.
- If *you* have a problem, it is *yours* to fix.
- If it is not *your* problem, don't own it!

QUESTIONS

- What do I criticise most in others?
- When do I do the thing I'm criticising in another? Is there a connection here?
- What criticisms are most often levelled at me?
- Is what I am most criticised for necessarily a bad thing?
- What should I do about what I am being criticised for?
- Is it in my *own* interests to change?

EXERCISE

Try role-playing with a friend before you have a difficult encounter with someone who is normally critical of you.

Try to identify the times when you react without thinking it through.

Aim to reach a solution satisfactory to *both* parties.

MY STORY

The most common criticism levelled at me over the years has been the one I have used as an example in this book - too sensitive.

When I finally began to see this sensitivity as an important component of my creativity and empathy with others, it ceased to be a problem and became a gift.

Nowadays, in the (now unlikely) event of receiving this criticism, my response, would be: `Hey, it's in the job description!'

Nearest and Dearest?

Working with intimate relationships

Now that you have begun recognising your blocks, it is time to take a fresh look at how they operate in an area where you are most likely to meet them head on ...

... with your

Nearest & Dearest!

Your Nearest and (possibly) Dearest may include your parents, your children, siblings, other family members, friends, and of course, your intimate partner.

For the purpose of this exercise, however, we will focus on your 'significant other' because, above all, this is where you come face to face with any unresolved pain, fear, anger, longings and, most importantly, your sense of self-worth.

- Who else pushes your buttons so effectively?
- Isn't this an arena for your greatest learning?
- Isn't this where your deepest resentments and resistances are played out?

Let's look –

In choosing our partners and friends, how often do we seek out the same kind of framework for affection that we experienced as children?

For instance, if your father was cold and distant, chances are you will choose partners who are similarly aloof and undemonstrative.

And, sure enough, you will feel just as **rejected** as you did in your childhood.

Why do we insist on returning to this pain?

Is this just our low opinion of ourselves?

Well, in order to understand this, let's do a bit of **brain surgery**!

The mind tends to operate on two different levels.

Introducing
Reasoning Brain ...

... and here, once again,
is **Primal Brain.**

The **Reasoning Brain** is the part we use most in daily life. It makes decisions, forms conclusions, deduces, calculates and rationalises.

The **Primal Brain's** main task is survival and self-preservation.

Here are the main attributes of these two levels of thinking.

REASONING BRAIN

- time-based
- aware of the five senses
- focused on one thing at a time
- prioritises where to focus attention
- makes choices about the way events are perceived.

PRIMAL BRAIN

- timeless (what was, still is)
- makes no distinctions between what is real or imagined (whatever **feels** true **will** be true)
- has no sense of humour
- works on anticipation or recollection of **sensations**
- seeks self-preservation and pleasure.

Lets look at them in action:

Here you are, happily using your **Reasoning Brain** to do your day's work.

Then, your **Reasoning Brain** remembers that `HE' is coming to pick you up. **PB** begins to give you warm, fuzzy feelings in response to the memory of HIM!

He hasn't arrived! You try calling. He's not there!

Reasoning Brain does its very best to kick in here - you **know** there are a million good reasons why he's late.

But it's no use. Old **Primal Brain** has zoomed straight back to childhood. You are five years old and you feel abandoned.

Primal Brain is recreating the environment of childhood, and hence, the same yearnings, and, as a result, the same pain.

Your suspicions were correct, your boyfriend is a notorious cheat and once again he's betrayed you?

Wait! Isn't **Primal Brain's** primary function **self-preservation**? Doesn't it seek out **pleasure?** Then what are you doing with ...

... THE LOVER FROM **HELL?!**

Well, old **PB** is not as masochistic as it may first seem ...

... It is actually **recreating** the hurts of childhood to **heal** the wounds and **resolve** unfinished business. It is seeking the pleasure of completion and wholeness. It is trying to reclaim the **BURIED SELF**

Let's see how this operates with **Romantic Love** ...

Along with the yearnings of **PB**, you begin your search ...

... you carry with you a mental checklist of qualities you find desirable ...

... many of these qualities will be a blend of your parents' qualities, and, interestingly, you will usually choose someone as attractive/intelligent/caring /honest, etc. as you **deem** yourself to be!

OK. So your eyes have met across a crowded room and all that stuff. It's love!

Actually, it's more like **lust** at this stage! Old **PB** is back with the dinosaurs and the search for a mate suitable for the continuance of the species *and* we're back to seeking out childhood nurture.

Anyway, it feels good! All the endorphins begin to fly around your system. The world looks great. You're smiling and happy.

Best of all, you feel better about *yourself*. Maybe you *are* adorable after all!

You're both now on your best behaviour. You are the perfect mate - caring, thoughtful, loving and kind ...

And, at first, you go to great pains not to be seem **needy**, but nurturing.

No wonder he loves you! You're so attentive, so giving and unselfish!

Well ... maybe. But in fact, in the end, you are there for your *own* needs, not your lover's, as you will see. This is about **PB**'s quest to heal *your* wounds, not his/hers.

Because, sure as eggs ...

... we start to care less about giving ...

... things change ...

... and more about **getting**

Trouble in Paradise!

Expectations become higher ...

... you find a multitude of faults you want to change in your partner ...

... and what was once endearing is no longer.

Suddenly, the man of your dreams has become Freddy Krueger!

SO WHAT HAPPENED?

Well, remember how you came to choose your partner?

In recreating your childhood, you have chosen a partner who reflects your parents' positive *and* negative traits - traits that you have also inherited!

Your partner serves as a mirror. What you like or don't like in your partner tend to be the things you like/don't like in yourself!

Sometimes, too, there can be a degree of wish fulfilment in your choice of partner, filling in the gaps you believe exist in your own personality.

If he's a **Party Animal** and you're retiring ... maybe you would actually like to be more outgoing!

However, # The Honeymoon's Over

At this stage, you've exhausted all the avenues. You've tried reasoning, bargaining, withholding and threatening, but there seems to be little hope.

But hold it for a second! Before you walk out, think about why you're in this relationship ...

TO HEAL YOURSELF !

Are the old patterns still in place?

Are they likely to repeat again even with a different partner?

Have you worked to resolve them in *this* relationship?

Perhaps a little more conscious work would help. Let's take a look:

GET OUT OF THE ILLUSION

This is *not* a fairytale. The hero is not here to fill your needs - that is *your* job!

Secondly, what you see is what you get! The person you met is going to remain the person you met, however much you want him/her to change!

No one can rescue another.

And the object of your desire who was meant to answer all of your prayers ...

... has just as much of the wounded child inside as you do!

ACCEPT THE DIFFERENCES
Be very clear about the person you see.

In what ways do they reflect *your* strengths and weaknesses, biases and qualities?

Accept differences between your characters as *essential*.

Your partner is not here to please or impress you, but to *grow* with you.

CO-OPERATE
Be clear that your purpose in being here is to heal yourself. Same for your partner.

When you hit a sticking point, **help** each other work it through. **Assist** each other in healing and growth.

OWN YOUR OWN STUFF
When something your partner does annoys or frustrates you, take a moment to look to yourself first.

- Why do you have difficulty in accepting this?
- What does this remind you of from the past?
- What **feelings** have surfaced?
- When do you do the same thing?
- Is this annoying because he/she is not living to *your* rules but his/hers?
- What is the **real** issue here?
- How would your partner be seeing it?

AND WHEN NONE OF THIS WORKS ... Let it go.

Accept the reality that this person cannot or will not love you in the way you want. Release him/her to be who he/she *actually is*. Stop allowing what you *can't* have to control your life. Let go.

QUESTIONS

- If you look back over your choice of partners, what pattern has been repeated?
- How do your partnerships reflect your relationship with your parents? In what ways are they significantly different?
- If your partners and friends are a reflection of you, what strengths and weaknesses do they reveal?
- What is your primary management style in relationships?

EXERCISE

Close your eyes and relax deeply. Bring up a picture of your loved one into your mind.

Try to **become** your loved one. Feel him/her breathing and imagine you are seeing through his/her eyes as he/she looks at you.

Try to see what your partner sees - what causes frustration, but also what is **loved** in you. Try to **understand** that both parts are **essential**. Both the unpleasant and the beautiful exist because you are you. And you are loved **for who you are**.

MY STORY

My relationship with my father was played out over and over through my life. Cool, distant and `difficult' men were attractive - nice guys were boring. My only understanding of affection was that you had to **struggle** for it.

That, of course, never worked. It took *years* to figure out that I deserved better, which was *my* lesson.

THAT WAS NO ACCIDENT!

The use of coincidence

I was just thinking about you!

- How often have you been thinking of someone you haven't seen for a long time, and out of the blue, they call you?

- How often have you worried that your money will not stretch when suddenly an unexpected cheque appears?

- How many major events in your life have been steered by a surprise turn of events?

Were these things just **COINCIDENTAL?**

When we see no order or pattern to our lives, we tend to perceive events as random - sometimes good luck comes our way, sometimes bad.

It was just chance!

Well, it certainly put you in the right place at the right time!

But if we take a broader view, we begin to see an interesting pattern within these apparent twists of fate, simply by being **CONSCIOUS** of them!

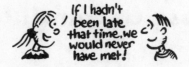
If I hadn't been late that time, we would never have met!

We tend to recall only major coincidences, but actually smaller `synchronicities' occur on a far more regular basis than we notice at first.

Interestingly — **THE MORE YOU WATCH FOR COINCIDENCES THE MORE THEY HAPPEN!**

If all we have to do is **tune in** to coincidences to have them occur more often
then surely ...

THEY MUST HAPPEN ANYWAY!

If we return to our list of possibilities, we find one that says
`**Everything happens for a reason**'.

If we can accept that our time on Earth is a schoolroom, then turns of events would function to position us in the right place at the right time for the greatest learning.

A higher level of freedom and control can arise from adopting the idea that we actually create our own circumstances.

HOW?

☆ Instead of feeling like helpless victims of **Fate**, we begin to look for the reasons for being in a particular situation and for what needs to be addressed in order to move on.

☆ We *go along* with events, rather than resisting and feeling stuck as a result.

☆ We begin to live life as an adventure, rather than an ordeal. We begin to examine events for clues and insights to use for growth and empowerment.

☆ We adopt a more expansive view of others, seeing them as instrumental to our own progress rather than sources of aggravation, frustration, pain or disempowerment.

☆ We accept more responsibility for what happens to us, rather than searching for someone or something to blame.

In fact, it could be said that, if all events have a purpose, then there *are* no **COINCIDENCES** or **ACCIDENTS** - only scene shifts, entrances and exits in the grand opera of life!

It could also be argued that coincidences or accidents are simply departures from the **expected outcomes** in any situation. Perhaps our subconscious is leading us in certain directions which coincide with the direction of others' subconscious and we intersect at certain points.

In any event, developing a consciousness of certain patterns in your life, relying on your intuition and becoming more aware of connections can serve as valuable tools for adding order to your life.

USING COINCIDENCE

Decision-making is one area in which taking note of linked or `fortuitous' connections can be very effective.

HOW TO DO THIS

1 CENTRE YOURSELF

Resist making decisions when you feel hurried, tired, angry or agitated. Wait for calm. There is *nothing* that can't wait if you think in terms of your whole life! (An exercise in letting go!)

2 TRUST YOUR INTUITION

3 PICTURE WHAT YOU WANT

Close your eyes and note what your inner voice tells you. Unlike the **IT** voice, your intuition will be in the form of a calm idea coming through. If the message is clear, heed it. If not, try again later. Learn to trust that you *have* wisdom and that you *will* get the answer.

We are often clearer on what we *don't* want than on what we *do* want! Visualise where you would like to be as a result of your decision. What is the outcome? Imagine it in full technicolour. Make it real.

4 START THE BALL ROLLING

Having worked out the direction you'd like to head in, begin to take **active steps** to set things in motion.

Write a letter, make a phone call, get a brochure, etc.

5 THEN, LET IT ROLL!

Now, sit back and simply watch what happens.

Notice how things unfold.

Is everything going smoothly?

Are there hitches? Are other possibilities coming through?

What are you seeing, hearing, reading, noticing in regard to your decision?

What clues are you getting?

CLUES

- Reading material
- Conversations
- Unusual mail, visits or phone calls
- `Chance' encounters
- Accidents
- Slogans, logos, graffiti
- Being delayed
- Arriving early
- Full bookings or sudden cancellations
- Trouble with machinery, car, phone, etc.
- Losing keys, wallet, etc.
- Encounters with strangers.

6 SURRENDER OUTCOMES

If it all goes like clockwork, **GREAT**! If not, if it's all terribly blocked ... **LET IT GO.** This is not always easy - especially if you had your heart set on something. But watch what arises as a result. Be **curious**, not cross!

Well, I tried all that and the outcome was a DISASTER!

Sorry to hear that. What happened?

I decided to move house. Everything went fine and I got the house I wanted.

Congratulations!

Yeah, right! I was burgled and mugged in the FIRST WEEK!!

Well sorry, I didn't guarantee happy endings, did I?

Well, no, but...

OK, I know it was tough. But what happened then?

Well, I did have insurance and...

And?

Well, after I was mugged, I started thinking about things.

Like?

Like, what's important, you know? I mean my LIFE had been in danger!

Yes. What did you decide?

I decided to finally move out of the city. I've always wanted to!

And how did that go?

Well, a friend happened to be selling his place and my insurance cheque came in, so I bought it!

And now?

Actually, I'm happier and more relaxed than I've ever been! I don't see possessions as being so important, either!

Thank you. I rest my case!

What is thrown at us can seem harsh or unfair at times, but essentially what you *need* may not be always what you *want*.

Our friend on the previous page *needed* to have his life endangered to fully recognise its worth. Most certainly, this would not have been what he *wanted*, but the impact was enough to completely change his attitude for the better.

Coincidences happen on many levels, but we tend only to recall those that seem to place us in a fortunate position, by our **existing standards**.

But misfortune in itself can, indeed, be fortunate, if the end result is a greater appreciation of who you are, and what you have.

Whether you stay **STUCK** in misfortune, or ride the waves of change and growth is up to you. But change is inevitable.

If only we had been brought up to value **CHANGE** more than we value **PERMANENCE**! How much more smoothly our lives would flow, if we were taught how to let go, move on, detach from outcomes and a belief in limited supply!

Instead of exhausting our energy shoring up against the uncertainties of tomorrow, we could be spending it on exploring the adventure of today!

And it **IS** an adventure!

Life can become **EXCITING**, a treasure hunt, when you begin to expect the unexpected!

Let's see what happens if you have a **PROBLEM**.

Say you've been having **huge hassles** with your boyfriend.

You've tried just about everything and right now you're completely confused about whether to stay and keep trying or to leave him, and get on with your life.

HERE'S WHAT TO DO.

1 ADMIT YOU'RE CONFUSED

I really don't know what's best!

When we keep pushing for a solution in a confusing situation, we can tend to become further buried in the problem. Give in! Admit you haven't got the answer ... **yet**.

3 WATCH WHAT HAPPENS

RING RING

2 GIVE IT AWAY

OK, whatever happens, I'll go with it!

Give away the outcome. Let things unfold as they will.

You might want to set a time limit on events - say by next week. Meanwhile get on with your life, **trusting** the answer will come.

Something will happen. The phone will ring, or there'll be a letter, or perhaps there will be silence, which will be a kind of answer in itself. You'll have your solution.

ABOUT ACCIDENTS

Accidents are usually wake-up calls.

You're bumbling along on some tangent that needs a shift in direction, or you need to be pulled up short to review the direction you're headed in.

Say you're at a dinner party. You're right in the middle of a story ...

... when suddenly, you spill wine all over your dress!

What were you about to say? Was it in your own best interests? If you could pick up the thread, would you? Does this warrant a rethink?

Accidents, especially those involving physical injury, are a means by which the psyche shocks you out of your trance, galvanising you into healthier action.

The more major the accident, the less you've been paying attention! There have probably been a lot of minor hints that you've been ignoring along the way, and its taken *this* to **wake you up.**

Accepting that you actually **create** what happens to you can feel rather confronting at first, but in time, you may recognise certain patterns of thinking that have accompanied events.

You may be equally surprised to find that, if you alter your thinking to a more positive outlook, you are less prone to illness or injury!

While some challenges appear in our life scripts to push us forward, we can sometimes pull other painful events toward us by our *own doing*.

It feels like an accusation to say that you `took part' in a crime perpetrated against you, or an apparent injustice that has befallen you.

But, I am relying on you to remain **open** in your thinking.

Let's put it this way-

This is *not* to say that you are to **blame** and the other party is **innocent.** But perhaps both of you were operating at the time on a **less conscious** level, which invited in this interplay.

Let's take a look-

Say you were the victim of violence.

- How is your self-worth?
- Do you live life believing that you are **fully worthy** of respect, love and happiness?
- Do you invest your trust in others wisely?
- Do you believe in life being hard?

If someone has stolen from you -

- Do you often feel `ripped off' by life?
- Do you find yourself feeling resentful that you are constantly giving more than you get in return?
- Are you overly concerned about losing possessions? Or ...
- Are you uncomfortable about being prosperous?

Being controlled by another or by events in any way, means that you have **allowed** yourself to **be controlled**.

This is a game, and your part in it **allows it to continue or not**.

DISENGAGE from the game and it will **stop**!

If you give too much - **stop**!

If you allow yourself to be bullied, put down, coerced, cheated – **stop**!

Sorry, I don't want to play anymore!

But this will require all of your courage to be **truthful** with yourself about the part that **you** play in what happens to you. Not easy!

You may have heard of **KARMA.** This is about **cause** and **effect.** It is not some mysterious Eastern concept. It makes sense. In other (Western) words

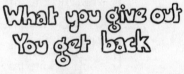

What you give out You get back

OR

What goes around comes around

Karma works in the following way. Whatever is unfinished, unresolved or incomplete will come around again until it is finished, resolved or completed.

It also means that whatever motives we use to acquire something, will be returned to us, in kind.

Say you cheat to get ahead.

Chances are you'll be cheated of your success or success will not bring joy.

It is a wonderful form of universal justice. If we take this on board, and someone *has* done wrong by us, we need do nothing to `get back'. At some stage they'll have to work it through. It is no longer your problem. No `revenge' is required.

MOTIVES AND RESPONSES

VIOLENT means - VIOLENT RESPONSES
RUTHLESS means - RUTHLESS RESPONSES
HELPFUL means - HELPFUL RESPONSES
SELFISH means - SELFISH RESPONSES
PEACEFUL means - PEACEFUL RESPONSES
And so on.

None of what you look at here is about **BLAME.** Questioning your role in events means that you are prepared to acknowledge your weaknesses in order to **LEARN** from them, **STRENGTHEN** them and **HEAL** them.

It means you are not a helpless puppet of **FATE**, but that you are a wonderful, complex human being who, with courage and honesty, is striving to grow!

QUESTIONS

- Under what circumstances did you meet your partner?
- Was your first `impression' an accurate one?
- How did you find your job, your house?
- Can you identify a part that you might have played in a recent disappointment or hurt?
- How might you act differently in the future?
- What happened the last time a different outcome arose from what you expected?

EXERCISE

Start trusting your hunches. The next time you feel `compelled' to do something, go with it, no matter how crazy it may seem.

Just see what happens, directly or indirectly, as a result of this hunch. A good rule is `intuition first, backed by logic'.

MY STORY

I had been waiting for an important phone call, but it seemed that it wasn't going to happen, because it was days overdue.

I set off on an errand, only to realise I'd left something behind. I returned home and put down my glasses while I collected the item I needed. Ready to leave again, I looked for my glasses. I *could not* find them. I searched and searched, becoming annoyed, when suddenly the phone rang. It was the phone call! As soon as I hung up, I walked past a chair and happened to notice my glasses had fallen behind a cushion!

MIND OVER MATTER

Changing
mental attitudes

Back to our list of possibilities again, and we find: 'What you **believe** will happen, will probably happen.'

Try this exercise:

1 Sit comfortably and slowly turn your head as far to the right as you possibly can.

2 As you do this, get a visual fix on something that is in line with the furthest point you can see.

3 Face the front again, close your eyes and, *without moving*, try to `feel' yourself turning your head *effortlessly past* the visual fix and all the way round till you are looking *behind* you!

4 Now, mentally turn your head till you face the front again, past the visual fix, *smoothly* and *easily*.

5 Now, open your eyes and repeat Step 1. How far past the visual fix did you get this time?

Wow! I can see the flowers

You'll be **AMAZED**!

So, what **happened**?

Quite simply, your reality was changed by **IMAGINING** that it was different!

By picturing yourself as being more flexible, you *became* more flexible!

This is the **POWER** of the mind. A power **you possess**!

Whatever you BELIEVE to be your reality will become your reality!

- If you **BELIEVE** life is tough, life *will* be tough!

- If you **BELIEVE** you'll always be broke, you'll *be* broke!

- If you **BELIEVE** you're limited, you'll *be* limited!

What do you **BELIEVE** about yourself? Do you **BELIEVE** you can have ...

- a totally equal relationship with someone who supports, respects, loves and nurtures you?

- a job that you enjoy going to each day?

- all the money you need without struggling?

- time to yourself, for yourself, completely free of demands?

- complete health and inner peace?

Can you see yourself having these things? What emotions come up around having what you dream of?

Is there even a kind of **PAIN** around having good things - being loved, being prosperous, being happy?

Is there a **FEAR** that if you allow in good things, they will only be ripped away?

Is struggle all you know, and therefore all you **BELIEVE** in?

Life *is* difficult, but how much *harder* are you doing it through your **BELIEFS** around a situation than the situation warrants?

Another item on our list of possibilities says:

`All suffering arises from our attitude to suffering.'

To demonstrate this, let's say you have something tough to go through. You can either –

Tell yourself over and over how hideous a situation is, thereby adding to your *own* difficulty in getting through it ...

OR

Take up the gauntlet and see the `hardship' as a task to be completed. Once you do this, the `suffering' goes out of it because you stop being a victim!

If you want a bad day, think this ...

GRANTED!
Today will be absolutely lousy! Enjoy!

Thoughts are powerful!

Here's another example of `Mind over Matter' -

Say there's something you'd rather not do, like writing that report you've been putting off ... **VS** Something pleasurable, such as lunch with the new receptionist!

On the appointed day, you wake up with a dreadful cold!

You feel lousy!

All morning, you struggle to keep going long enough to write the report ...

... but amazingly, by lunchtime, the symptoms are just a minor irritation!

We've all done it! But what's the difference here? You're still sick, but one situation has you feeling worse than the other.

It's when we **BELIEVE** something is onerous, painful, fearful, overwhelming or disabling, that it becomes so!

THE UGLY DUCKLING

Another powerful trick of the mind involves self-image.

When you look in the mirror, what do you see?

Do you immediately zoom in on the flaws?

If you perceive yourself as flawed, you are likely to project this. But if you think of yourself as beautiful, an interesting thing happens ... you actually **become more attractive**!

Let's see this in action.

If you believe you are flawed, you begin to close in on yourself.

You are more likely to stoop, frown, look tense and unhappy.

You try to compensate for or cover your faults with various devices of posture, make-up, clothing, etc., hoping no one will see your faults.

You become self-conscious and guarded.

But what happens if ...

Someone falls in love with you?

Someone thinks you're wonderful, beautiful, sexy, whatever, **just as you are**!

An interesting transformation occurs.

You actually become **MORE ATTRACTIVE**! Your gestures become more expansive, you have more energy, your expression softens and you smile more.

What if, instead of someone else doing this for you, you did it for **YOURSELF**?

Simply by recognising beauty in yourself, you allow the potential for that beauty to shine through.

Even smiling more, or being conscious of relaxing *your* face, can have a big impact, both on the outside *and* the inside. Research has shown that smiling actually calms us emotionally.

And this brings us to HUMOUR!

Have you forgotten how to **play**? Has it all become so dire, so serious that you've forgotten to fit **fun** in there? Enlightenment can also mean to simply **lighten up**! Laughter and fun on a regular basis can be a far greater healer than any prescription!

Life can be joyous! **Seek out** the joy.

How much time do you spend rerunning the **pain** in your memory, keeping it alive?

What happened to all the good times? Weren't they just as real, just as valid?

Stop being so **EARNEST**. Goof around, play the fool, see the great cosmic joke of it all. Life's a game, an adventure. See the bummers as perfect **SLAPSTICK**, a big banana peel, or a cream pie in the face!

AUTOMATICALLY OK

To significantly change how you feel, you will need to become an expert at self-observation. If you don't, you get caught up in knee-jerk, mechanical reactions.

Be especially watchful for old patterns of thinking creeping back in.

By now, you will have, hopefully, done a lot of monitoring of your self-talk through the work covered in *Living with IT* and *Living IT Up*. If so your vocabulary ...

will no longer include these ...

• SHOULD   • EVER
• CAN'T   • ALWAYS
• MUST   • NO-ONE
• NEVER   • EVERYONE
• NOTHING   • EVERYTHING

... and you will have replaced them with these.

• COULD   • RARELY
• COULD/CAN   • MOSTLY
• PREFER TO   • FEW PEOPLE
• SELDOM   • MOST PEOPLE
• FEW THINGS   • MOST THINGS

By now your **AUTOMATIC** choice will be **self-supporting**. If not, practise until it is.

Also remove -

• SELF-CRITICISM
• CRITICISM OF OTHERS
• ACCUSATIONS
• ULTIMATUMS
• UNREQUESTED ADVICE
• SERMONS
• 'NO I DON'T'
• 'I DO SO'
• 'YOU DID X'

And replace with -

• SELF APPROVAL
• ACCEPTANCE
• PERSONAL REFLECTION
• REQUESTS
• NON-INTERFERENCE
• HUMILITY
• 'I DON'T AGREE'
• 'I SEE IT DIFFERENTLY'
• 'I FEEL Y WHEN YOU DO X'

And remember - you can only hold **ONE THOUGHT** at a time!

MAKE IT A GOOD ONE!

QUESTIONS

- What things do you **believe** you can have in life?
- How many of your goals have you managed to fulfil?
- How likely do you think it is that they will be fulfilled in your lifetime?
- When you look in the mirror, what is the first thing you notice?
- How many times have you been playful or used humour in the last twenty-four hours?

EXERCISE

Keep a tab on how many times you use the words should, must and can't in one week.

Make a note of the situation you used the word to describe.
How could you reassess this?

MY STORY

Writing *Living with IT* was the best therapy I could have. In choosing to use humour as a means of illustrating such a painful experience for my readers, I was, in turn, re-evaluating the very nature of my **IT**. Because I could laugh (no matter how nervously) at my troubles, **IT** began to be `naughty' rather than sinister. I started to see **IT** as he was, my unruly child needing discipline and focus.

LETTING GO AND HANGING
IN THERE

**Release
and
perseverance**

It's easier to apply all of the principles that we've looked at when things are going smoothly. But when things get tough, most of what we know is best for us goes out of the window.

That's when you need to **LET GO** and **HANG IN THERE**.

LETTING GO

Let's look at this script of yours again. This scene opens at tragedy, or at least a major drama.

Whether this goes on page after page is not up to luck, but **how you choose to handle the situation.**

Often we get caught up in suffering because it makes us so damned **interesting**!

Have you noticed how people actually compete to have the greatest suffering? We do this because it offers perverse rewards.

Primal Brain (remember old **PB**?) is in action here. Remember how, as a child, if you were upset or hurt you were held, cuddled, stroked?

- Suffering makes us noticeable.
- Suffering gets us attention.
- Suffering brings us the nurturing we crave.

The trouble is, if this is the *ONLY* way we believe we can be noticed or loved, it becomes a **profession**!

IT'S TIME TO MOVE ON!

Why? Because the attention that you may get out of suffering, instead of bolstering you, actually **DISEMPOWERS** you. You stay locked in a cycle of feeling helpless while being treated as helpless. You **give away** your power.

LET'S LOOK AT TWO KEY POINTS:

1 LIFE IS NOT EASY
Really get this.

> LIFE IS NOT EASY

   GROWTH is in your script. That's it. No happy endings, no sailing off into the sunset. You may have tough challenges all your life, if you have to clear a lot of stuff, or you may have a holiday cruise.

BUT (BIG BUT!)

The more you grow, the less you see situations as intolerable. You **seek out** the good buried within the situation. You **stop resisting** and **resenting** and **get cracking**. Therefore, as a result ...

> You experience LESS PAIN!!

Within every situation there is an equal potential for `good' or `bad'.
It's how you **see** it. It's the **memory** of pain that keeps it alive!

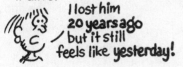

I lost him 20 years ago but it still feels like yesterday!

How **often** do you tell your sad story? How long will you keep it **alive**?

Your suffering can only last as long as the time you spend recalling it!

2 YOU CREATE YOUR OWN REALITY

Mr Sad, Mr Bleagh and Mr Joy are all neighbours.

Mr Sad, Mr Bleagh and Mr Joy's houses are all wiped out in a bushfire.

They have all lost everything, including a family member.

They have all shared an equal tragedy.

But what differs is **the way each handles it!**

It's my fault! I should have saved her!

It's their fault! They should have saved her!

Mr Sad lives out the rest of his life in guilt and remorse. He blames himself.

Mr Bleagh, meanwhile, blames others and the authorities. He remains in a bitter rage.

Mr Joy decides to work with others who have had a similar loss. Through this he finds a purpose for his own suffering.

What would YOU choose?
You can **choose** to hold on to a situation or move on, having gained valuable insights.

Oh I can't have THAT!

How much **JOY** do you feel you deserve?

How much are you prepared to do to feel better? **ANYTHING**?

Then, it's time to **SIMPLIFY** your life. It's time to **LET GO**!

Let go, Let go of... - a little more each day.

ANGER

Anger impacts on **you**. It keeps you locked into the past. It makes **you** the victim as much as the person you are angry with! Refuse to keep calling up the thought of what you're angry about.

What if I feel BAD?

FEAR

Fear is always **future-based**. It arises from **anticipation**. It consists of a **present** decision to feel a certain way in the **future**! For instance, if you fear rejection, you've decided to feel **rejected already**! You could choose another reaction!

I'm too wittle to do dat!

ENFEEBLEMENT

How often do you accept limitations? I'm too little, too lost, too confused, too stupid, too weak, too sick, too scared, too old, too this, too that? Who says? **You** do!

Let go, Let go of...

> **RULES**
> **GAMES**
> **INSINCERITY**
> **TRYING TO PLEASE**
> **PUNISHING YOURSELF**
> **BLAMING**
> **CRITICISM**
> **GUILT**
> **DENIAL**
> **EXPECTATIONS**

Let go till you feel yourself get lighter!

And, sometimes, when the going gets tough, all you can do is

HANG IN THERE!

As we've seen, growing through challenges requires accepting that they are an inevitable part of this growth.

The other part is *how* you work through them. If you do it kicking and screaming, you'll still go *through the challenge* only you'll do it **twice as hard!**

Sometimes things *do* feel almost unbearable. But somehow we *do* bear them, and we usually emerge the better for it, especially if we don't run, but **HANG IN THERE!**

And, to **HANG IN THERE**, you will need to become a kind of

WARRIOR

You have something tough to do, so it's best to get on with it and get it over with.

So, if you were a **WARRIOR**, what qualities would serve you best?

Oh dear, I'm not sure... maybe, but then...

1 DISCIPLINE

What is a warrior without discipline? A warrior has to undergo training to succeed, and **discipline** to apply this training under pressure. Discipline yourself to think better, watch what you say, and to get out of the knee-jerk reactions. Apply yourself.

2 DIGNITY

Hold your head up. Be a **proud** warrior! Don't fall for tactics that belittle you. Treat yourself and others with respect. Know you have strength, courage, wisdom. Give up complaining, nagging, blaming, regretting. It's beneath you!

3 DETACHMENT

Become a curious onlooker to events, rather than allowing them to overwhelm you.

Observe situations from the perspective of an onlooker. Be objective.

Take time to consider reactions and responses before applying them.

Keep a cool head.

4 HONOURING YOUR OWN JUDGEMENT

You know what's best for *you*, no one else. You don't need anyone else's advice or opinions. You know what to do. If not, find out. Do not rely on *anyone* else's wisdom. That's theirs. Find *yours*.

5 ACTION

Theory is fine, but it doesn't get things done. A simple equation is: Time plus inaction = no results. Strap on your sword and **act** to change things for the better.

6 PERSEVERANCE

You may find that you have to hang in there for quite a while: OK. Just do it **ONE DAY AT A TIME.** Even one **hour** at a time if you have to. *It will take as long as it takes.* Forget about when it will end. You'll know when it has. Keep going till then. Never yield one victory! Never compromise what you've fought to gain!

7 INDEPENDENCE

Learn to rely on yourself to provide what you need. Do not rely on others to entertain, amuse, love, support, heal or nurture you. Others may not be able to provide these things when you need them, but you can.

Find them in yourself, first.

8 FREEDOM FROM DOUBT

A warrior relies on an unwavering conviction that he/she is strong enough, wise enough, and has enough of what it takes to succeed. Without this, the warrior will fall. Trust that all is exactly as it should be. Trust that you will be OK. I know it's been hard, very hard, but you must be strong indeed if you have been given big challenges!

It's like any game of skill - the better you get, the higher the degree of difficulty!

YOU'RE A WINNER!

QUESTIONS

- What is there in your life that you have trouble letting go of?
- What would happen if you did?
- How often in the past week have you talked about a problem?
- When faced with an ongoing difficulty, are you able to focus on the present, or do you visualise the problem going on and on into the future?

EXERCISE

Here is a very effective exercise to clear old anger and grief.

When you are alone and unlikely to be disturbed, stand in the centre of a room. Face one end and call into your mind all of the hurt, fear, anger, pain and sadness that you have known in your life. Really **feel** it, and let the emotions come. Cry if you need to.

When you feel you have cleared this, imagine that all of this pain is lying in a heap before you. Now wrap it up in a big parcel, tie it with string, and throw it away. That is the past. It is over.

Now turn and face the other end of the room. That is the future. Step forward and embrace it.

MY STORY

Whenever it all gets too much, I often call on the warrior idea, and, just by straightening up into that proud stance, I find the extra strength I need. When I find myself whingeing, whining or weeping, I suddenly remember the warrior, and I can't imagine her wasting one second on self-pity, like that.

THE PEACE PIPE

Applying love
and forgiveness

If you return once more to the possibilities on page 18, you will find the last one says `Love is an antidote to all suffering'.

How can love ease suffering?

What's **LOVE** got to do with it, when all seems unfair, uncaring or when others seem callous to our pain or, at times, even seem to add to it?

Here's what.

Why should I be loving when no one shows love to me??!

YOU'LL FEEL BETTER!

Let's get something straight. **REAL LOVE** is not for the **FAINT-HEARTED**. The benefits of a loving attitude can only come from **HONESTY, CLARITY** and **DISCIPLINE.**

AND REAL LOVE takes **COURAGE.**

Here's the other one!

It does not mean:

- lying down and playing dead
- turning a blind eye to reality
- being `nice'
- becoming a saint
- stepping out of the everyday world.

Why does everyone walk over me?

La la, everything's sooo beautiful!!

Adopting a loving perspective in many ways means simply **LOSING RESISTANCE!**

For example:

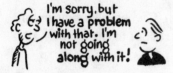

It means being **ASSERTIVE** *without* introducing **ANGER!**

It means **BEING CLEAR** in asking for what you *need* without playing **CONTROL** games to get it!

It means that you do not have to be **DEFENSIVE** because you've stopped perceiving **ATTACK!**

It means that, by applying patience, acceptance and empathy, instead of just **reacting**, you learn to **RELAX** about coping with 'difficult' situations.

It means loving yourself and others enough to cease **controlling** by caretaking, fixing or rescuing others. It means attending to *yourself* first, so that you, too, do not impinge on others, and so that you *can* be strong and helpful if you are called on.

APPLYING LOVE INVOLVES:

- ♥ **caring** about everything you do
- ♥ leaving others alone
- ♥ **valuing** what you have
- ♥ taking **care** of yourself
- ♥ giving without conditions
- ♥ being **sincere**
- ♥ **accepting**
- ♥ **never assuming** someone has fewer feelings than you
- ♥ allowing others to be **exactly** who they are
- ♥ relinquishing judgement
- ♥ having **dignity**
- ♥ having **humility**
- ♥ investing **trust** wisely

Let's look at some of these:

♥ CARING AND VALUING

We take so much for granted. The fact that we have a life at all is pretty amazing when you think about it. And this incredible, complex, self-correcting body that carries us around warrants a moment's pause for thought. **Love** life. **Care** about it, and how you use this gift.

♥ LEAVING OTHERS ALONE

Honour another person's lessons as being their own. If you think they're making a mistake, **let them**. That's how *you* learned! Can you really say you've got it *all* figured out yourself?

♥ GIVING UNCONDITIONALLY

Give only when you expect nothing back. If you find yourself doing something for someone out of duty or obligation instead of a true desire to, you'll carry resentment with you. And that is *not* giving.

♥ BEING SINCERE

Not being true to yourself, and not being sincere to others rips you and them off. Sincerity means stepping out and revealing your true feelings, faults, strengths, doubts, etc. without games.

♥ ACCEPTING

This means that you accept where you are, how things are and others **AS THEY ARE**. Just go with it all. It's **MEANT TO BE** like this.

♥ FEELINGS

Being loving means identifying the fellow human being within. We're all just frightened little kids inside, trying to get by. You are, he is, she is. All we want is for *someone* to give a damn.

♥ HUMILITY

This means acknowledging you're not perfect and that's OK! It also means getting out of saying `I know'. Be open to the possibility that you don't ...**YET**.

♥ INVESTING TRUST

Basically, to keep walking back into pain doesn't mean you're being more loving ... it means you're being self-punishing! Loving another doesn't mean throwing away love for *yourself*!

And, of course, the most **LOVING** thing to do is to

OK. So you feel you have been wronged and, indeed, maybe someone *has* done something pretty lousy to you. What do you do?

Say your best friend has **stolen** from you ...

you trusted her and she broke your trust. At first you are shocked, then sad ...

... then you get **MAD**!

You decide you will *never ever* forgive her for what she did!

From now on, she **doesn't exist.** You will *never* speak to her again. She's **out**! She'll **never** get the chance to hurt you again!

Guess who you think about **ALL THE TIME**! The very person you want out of your life!

Month after month, year after year, the anger eats at **YOU**!

There's only one cure ...

FORGIVE HER!

What ?? NEVER!!

WAIT! I didn't say that you should make up with her, or even see her (walking back into pain is dumb, right?). Just **FORGIVE** her.

Why should I do that? It's her fault!

Maybe. But **YOU'RE** the one who's **suffering**!

Take a look at what **not forgiving** does to **YOU** ...

PAST

You become a **PRISONER** of the **PAST**. You constantly rerun the old movie about who did what. You cause **yourself** pain.

You are immobilised. Stuck in the **PAST,** you remain blind to the **PRESENT** and can't get on with the future.

What's wrong?

You are stuck in a **PATTERN**.
Because you have not forgiven (i.e. let go) you look for similar treachery in others.
You no longer allow the trust that ensures closeness to others. If you stay in a rage, you screen out the chance to **REBUILD** that trust.

Unreleased anger has a lasting effect on *you* physically and emotionally, causing muscle tension, restless sleep, poor digestion, etc.

Can you see it is in your own interests to **FORGIVE**?

HOW TO FORGIVE

Most of what we have already covered comes into play here. Here's a refresher:

1 DIFFERENT SCRIPTS

It was in your script that your friend would betray you. *Why?*
Did you invest your trust unwisely?
Did your friend need help?
What did you need to learn about friendship and possessions?
What was in your friend's script?

2 MEMORY SELECTION

What you **CHOOSE to REMEMBER** will affect how you feel. No one walks around full of anger unless they keep calling up the **MEMORY** of anger.
You have the choice to feel better by letting the issue go. If **you** choose to hold the pain, then that should tell you something!

3 COMPASSION

A person who does a mean thing is not a person who feels good about him/herself. Compassion is about seeing past the act, to the sadness/ anger/ loneliness that prompted it. See others as two types - those who extend love and those who need it.

FORGIVENESS is an act of love for yourself and others that **FREES** you and others to move on. The sooner you get to forgiveness, the sooner you get to **PEACE**.

FORGIVING YOUR PARENTS

This is a special case. Your parents *should* have provided you with nurture, love and security. If they did not, the wounds will run very deep.

HOW CAN WE HEAL THIS?

1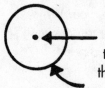
Well, say you are the dot in the centre of this circle ...

... and the rest of the circle represents your potential to be loving, whole and strong. In other words, your potential for spiritual development.

2
During your lifetime, by working at it, you may manage to fulfil your spiritual potential to this level.

3
Your parents (and others) for various reasons (economic, social, political, etc) may have only made it *this* far.

4
So, it figures you will need to be **EXPANDED** enough to embrace their limited realised potential, like this.

So this means asking yourself, how can I be **BIG** enough to accommodate this?

One way of doing this is to recognise what you have **LEARNED** from your parents. Did the **LIMITATIONS** of your childhood push you towards overcoming these limitations in your own adulthood?

Out of a determination *not* to repeat your parents' mistakes did you become ...

More loving?

More creative?

Less 'driven'?

Yes! I can do that!

More determined?

But the one you need to forgive most is ...

YOURSELF

Forgive Yourself for ...

Not being perfect ... *no one* is!

Making mistakes ... that's how you **LEARN**!

The bad things you have done ...

... or that have been done to you.

And, even for the **GOOD THINGS** ...

... you don't believe you *deserve*.

If you *did* act badly, **FORGIVE YOURSELF** by:

- identifying *why* you acted badly
- healing what lies behind the thing you did
- rectifying the situation
- not repeating it in the future.

FORGIVE YOURSELF for being just what you are: a complex, intricate, unique **HUMAN BEING** trying to grow.

QUESTIONS

- What do you feel guilty about? Have you forgiven yourself?
- Who do you still need to make peace with?
- What steps could you take to do this?
- Ask yourself, in a difficult situation: `What would be the *loving* thing to do?'
- How loving (to yourself and others) have you been today?

EXERCISE

LOVE: One of the most loving acts is to **LISTEN** to another. Most times we're only *half* listening.

How to listen
- Do not interrupt.
- Do not judge anything you hear as right, wrong, stupid, etc.
- Do not give *any* feedback unless asked (even uh huhs or yeses introduce *your* stuff).
- Let the person speak until they have said all they want to.
- Learn to be comfortable with silence.

FORGIVENESS: Write down the name of someone you need to forgive. Say three times: `X, I forgive you, from the bottom of my heart. I set you and myself free from my anger. Go in peace.' Repeat this exercise until you truly feel free of anger or resentment.

MY STORY

I was with a friend who was having a lot of trouble socially. She was often accused of rudeness and indeed, when stressed, she could be `difficult' - easily annoyed, irritable and short with others.

As she related her latest frustration with a colleague, she began to become agitated and angry. Purely on a hunch, I decided to try love. I cleared my mind of judgement and tried to see past her anger to the pain that caused it. Then, centring myself, I told her mentally that I loved her. Immediately she stopped mid-sentence, hesitated, then said, suddenly calmer, `I've forgotten what I was saying!' Amazing!

THE
GETTING
OF
WISDOM

AHA!

Strategies
for
developing awareness

No matter how many books you read, theories you adopt, ideas you formulate or discussions you have, **WISDOM** can come to you only through **direct experience**, and through this experience becoming your **personal truth**.

 First, there is **information** ...  ... and when this information becomes material that you apply to your own life, it becomes **knowledge** ...

AHA!

... and when this knowledge is put into **practice** in your life, it becomes your own **WISDOM**.

The next time you hear yourself saying ...

I know that!

... ask yourself - Am I **living** it? If you still apply anger, fear, judgement, defence or control to be acknowledged, nurtured or supported, then probably you *don't* know ... YET.

Only when you...

WALK YOUR TALK

are you living your wisdom

You may encounter the same notion over and over till *finally* it clicks into place.

Something brings this concept into the realm of your personal experience and brings it home.

'Don't judge others'... Well I don't. Not like Muriel, she ...

Whoops! I was judging Muriel!

NOW I get it!

It has become your personal **truth**.

FOR EXAMPLE:

When you actually apply forgiveness to someone who has hurt you ...

... or you stop yourself just as you were about to join in on gossip about someone ...

... or you stop being **OBSESSIVE** about that deadline ...

... or you take the time to be fully **present** for another ...

... and you experience a kind of freedom from this, a letting go inside, a clean, clear feeling ...

YOU'VE GOT IT!

And as a result, the next time you experience the old thinking, you'll *feel* the contrast.

These `flashbacks` - when you catch yourself up to your old tricks again - can be humbling and sometimes painful.

But they serve as reminders of *old* pain, that you are now working to clear.

So, how can you **access this wisdom**? Well, first of all, it means getting **BALANCE** back into your life.

A good way to do this is to allocate adequate time each day for the following:

WORK   STUDY
REST   and
PLAY   SPIRITUAL PRACTICE

Let's look ...

Work is important, but are you working to live or living to work? If work consumes your whole life, what is it about your **life** that isn't working?

How much time do you give yourself to shut down, switch off and tune out each day? Isn't loving yourself about giving your body and mind time out to recharge?

Go ahead! Be **silly** at least once a day. Giggle, tickle, roar around, be a big kid. Do you **play** enough?

Or perhaps you play too hard. Again, **BALANCE**. Whether this is about exercise, entertainment, socialising or whatever, take a fresh look. How do you do this?

STUDY

SPIRITUAL PRACTICE

You have the most interesting subject on earth ... **YOURSELF**. If you want to change the way you think, compare it with what others think.

Try on new ideas, explore, open up to new knowledge. Read a book, discuss a theory, see a counsellor, begin a journal or just have a think.

You may find spiritual nurture in watching a sunset or sitting in a garden. Or you may connect more strongly through prayer, meditation or a discipline like yoga. Fifteen minutes a day away from physical concerns, thinking peaceful or uplifting thoughts - that's all it takes to make a difference: to connect you with your higher self and a higher purpose.

Here are some practices that will keep you focused.

1 A BOOK OF WISDOM

Start a little book of lessons. At the end of each day, ask yourself: `What did I **learn** today?' Perhaps you read something inspirational or you had an insightful conversation or pivotal encounter. Try to pinpoint the theme of the day and your understanding of it. For example: `**RESPONSIBILITY -** others are not the cause or the cure of my problems.'

2 A JOURNAL

Keeping a journal is like having a confidante, best friend and counsellor at hand any time of the day. Use your journal to express and clear your feelings, thoughts, longings, dreams and problems. Make it a safe place to work through your deepest issues. Only you need know what it contains, and when you look back at it later, you will be encouraged by this evidence of your own progress.

3 A QUESTIONNAIRE

If you feel blocked or stuck in a problem, or feel upset without really knowing why, work it through by creating a personal questionnaire. Allow your questions and their responses to flow out as automatically as you can. You'll know when you've reached the heart of the matter. You may find yourself crying a little when you hit the spot. This is fine. You will be releasing whatever is blocking you, and feel lighter as a result.

POSSIBLE QUESTIONS
- What do I feel?
- How am I blocked?
- What would make me feel better?
- What can I do to feel better?
- In what way am I holding this block in place?

4 SEEK A QUIETER MIND

Understanding a problem may be helpful, but understanding is only *part* of healing. Working too hard intellectually at being `wise' can often remove you from the very source of your own wisdom - your inner guidance. Only when you quieten down the din of thinking can your true **WISDOM** be heard. The seeking of a peaceful mind and a peaceful approach to life in itself solves most problems!

5 HEALING THE HURT CHILD

 All the reasoning in the world will not stop the emotions of your hurt inner child rising in certain situations. A button gets pressed that jet-propels you back to your earliest feelings of fear, abandonment, denial, etc. Well into adulthood, that hurt child will still throw tantrums, sulk, whinge, cringe or wail. The only one who can heal him/her is you. Contact the child inside. Pour all the love he/she lacked onto him/her. Talk kindly and gently to the child. Heal the wounds. Then let the child go.

6 GIVE IT AWAY

If you haven't got enough of something - love, attention, even money - give away some of what you *do* have.

It's a bit like clearing a blocked drain to allow the natural flow of things to resume. The block you are clearing is your own `closing down' around your problem. In performing this act of giving, you **open up** to the possibility of receiving what you lack. In essence, you are saying `I'll **trust** that if I let go of this, more will come in to replace it.' See what happens!

And, finally, there are two age-old rituals guaranteed to connect you to the spiritual and your inner wisdom:

MEDITATION AND PRAYER

MEDITATION

 We looked at meditation in some detail in *Living* **IT** *Up*.

In essence, meditation allows you to reach a still point in yourself that removes you from the clutter of thoughts, cares, and demands of daily life and allows your own peaceful wisdom to arise naturally.

PRAYER

Like meditation, prayer teaches stillness, trust and release.

However, while meditation focuses you on an inward level, prayer operates on an **active outward affirmation.**

In offering up a prayer, we set up, in our own minds, the possibility of a solution, a resolve or a change of thinking necessary to move along a current situation.

So prayer operates on a **psychological** level as well as a **spiritual** level.

PRAYER WORKS!

But only if you have **FAITH** that it will work!

FAITH means trusting that whatever is needed will come, that you **surrender control** of an outcome and **allow** things to unfold as they will, and go along with it all.

This can mean, of course that things may work out differently to what you might expect! There's a popular joke that demonstrates this:

128

BUT THE FLOOD WATERS RISE AND THE MAN DROWNS!

ARRIVING IN HEAVEN, HE PROTESTS TO GOD...

But I was sure You'd come and rescue me!

AND GOD REPLIES...

Blimey! I sent you a ROWBOAT, a CHOPPER & a MOTOR LAUNCH! What _more_ did you want?!

What this means is that we need to be open to what *is* available to us, without getting fixed on something else.

In this sense, a desperate, angry or frustrated prayer is likely to go 'unanswered', because your desperation, anger or frustration will blind you to the sources of help that may be available to you.

HOW TO PRAY

Say you want more money. That's OK. Money can mean the difference between struggle and a sense of freedom. But think

about it. Is it the money or the **feeling** that goes with having enough money that you long for? Would it make you feel more secure, less stressed? Would it mean you could relax?

THAT'S what to pray for!

The FEELING   The THINKING
The HEALING   The LETTING GO ...

If you're upset ...   If you're worried ...   If you're lonely ...

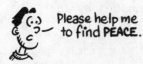

Please help me to find PEACE.

Please let me THINK RIGHT about this.

Please help me feel LOVED.

... getting that new car may not bring you any joy at all!

Praying for **RESCUE** won't work either. Who is going to rescue you, except *yourself*? Most times, like our friend on the roof, the only danger we need to be rescued from is ourselves and our limited, negative thinking!

ANSWERS TO PRAYERS

Sit back and **TRUST** that what you need is on its way. All the strength, focus, patience, love and wisdom that you need is on its way ... **if** you **let it**!

OPPORTUNITY MAY KNOCK OVER AND OVER BUT IF THE DOOR IS LOCKED AND BOLTED HOW CAN IT GET IN ??

Phooee! It doesn't work!!

This means that if you stay locked in anger, fear, whatever, without **letting in** the possibility of feeling better, you'll stay exactly where you are ... **FEELING BAD**!

PRAYING FOR OTHERS

How can you stay **mad** at someone at the same time that you're sending them good thoughts through prayers?

This is a way of clearing and forgiving. It helps both *you* and others. Prayer can also be used to send help in your absence. Your prayer is a means of sending positive energy to someone in need of it, and, in this giving, you allow more to flow back to you.

Can you see now how prayer combines **all** that is on our list of **POSSIBILITIES**?

Be still, **TRUSTING** that your prayer is heard, by whoever or whatever you wish to direct it to ... God, a Divine Force or your Higher Self. Then, stay tuned.

QUESTIONS

- What is your spiritual practice for each day?
- How much time do you allocate in your life for peaceful, uplifting thoughts?
- How well do you know your own psychology?
- Would you benefit from getting more **peace** in your life?
- What active steps could you take to do this?

EXERCISE

Try asking for the **right words** in your dealings with others.

Just before answering the phone, talking to a friend or relative (especially `difficult' people), attending a meeting or visiting a client, take a moment to centre yourself around letting exactly the right words flow through you during this exchange with another. See what happens.

MY STORY

Like many people, I had for a long time a real problem with the idea of praying. It brought back less than comforting memories of the church and religion in my earlier years, which I had turned my back on. However, like many people, I still resorted to prayer when I found myself in a crisis. In time, I realised that it wasn't prayer that was the problem, but more the expectations I had of it and its connotations for me. Now I realise that all I asked for has been granted to the degree that I have **allowed** these things to be granted.

AMEN

OVER IT

YIPPEE!!

Summary

Whew! We've covered a lot of territory! Time to put it all together, eh?

Let's look at how all this might operate in three different versions of a situation.

Here's Betty ...   ... and here's John.

Neither John nor Betty have done much of the work that appears in this book. They're just going along, not terribly unhappy, but not terribly happy either, like most people. They've never met, but they're about to ...

SMASH!!

... HEAD ON!

And, like most people, this is how they **react** ...

You weren't watching where you were going!!

WHAT??! You came straight at me!!

Oh yeah?! Well, you were in the wrong lane!

Oh come on! It's your fault! AND now you've made me miss an important appointment!

Well, you'll be hearing from my lawyers!!

Not before you hear from MINE!

Now, let's say JOHN and BETTY are **NOT** strangers!

Are you **all right**?

Yes, I'm fine! Are you?

Yes, I'm OK. But this is a mess, eh?

Yeah. Look, what do you think happened?

Well, I went to change lanes and all I saw was you coming at me!

Hmm, changing lanes...THERE?! Well, I guess it's over to the insurance companies to sort out!

Hmm, well they're **NOT QUITE** blaming, but... Now here's a version where Betty and John have done some **NEW THINKING**...

Well, I'm glad we're both **OK**! Too bad about the cars!

Yeah. Pretty interesting that we both needed such a jolt, though!

Well, I had a tiff with my husband this morning. I guess I was still carrying some **anger**!

I guess you've let it out now!

Sure have!

And I was on my way to a meeting I really didn't want to go to!

Well, you got out of that!

Well, kind of... but it will probably be rescheduled. No avoiding it!

Well I'd better ring John. **This** may bring things to a **head**, but we need to sort things through!

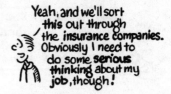

Yeah, and we'll sort this out through the insurance companies. Obviously I need to do some **serious** thinking about my job, though!

Wouldn't it be **great** if we all responded in this way? Why **don't** we?

BECAUSE

- We perceive others as **separate** from us. What's the saying? `A stranger is a friend you haven't met yet!' What if we were just as caring and compassionate towards those people we don't know as to those we do?

- We hang onto things. `But I worked hard for that car!' But it's a *car*. *You* are alive! You'll get another, or you'll take the bus and who knows what *that* will bring!

- We fear scarcity. `How will I ever pay for this?' I don't know. But you will. Think about it. Don't you always manage?

- We see events as outside our control. When Betty admitted to her anger and John to his problem with the meeting, they took responsibility and absolved each other of blame. Even if we can't come at the idea that we *caused* the accident, we could look at whether we were distracted or focused elsewhere.

Life gets simpler when you own what happens to you because *you* get to sort out what happens next!

Well, the world's been operating a certain way for a long time and, let's **face it**, there's room for some new thinking!

It may seem a bit lofty to imagine that by getting your own act together, you can make changes on a global scale!

But what if enough people made the changes you have~ if they became more aware, loving, peaceful, forgiving~ if they feared each other less...

... surely it would have to have some effect! A better world... imagine! Hey! ANYTHING'S POSSIBLE...

... and everything happens for a **REASON** and, who knows... maybe that's

IT !!